THE SOROS LECTURES

GEORGE SOROS

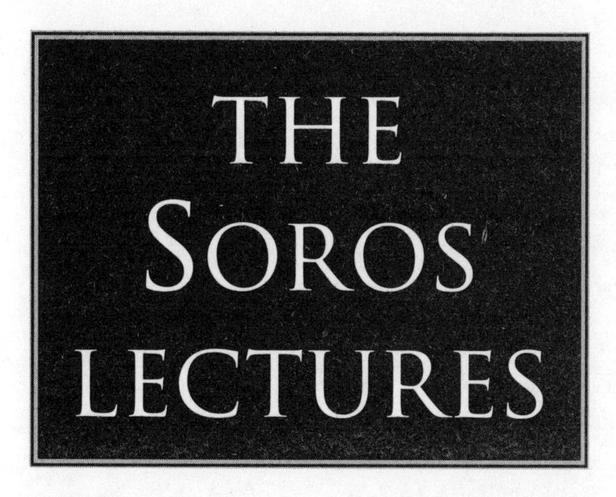

AT THE CENTRAL EUROPEAN UNIVERSITY

PUBLICAFFAIRS *New York*

Published in the United States by PublicAffairs™, a member of the Perseus Books Group.

Printed in the United States of America.

Book Design by Jenny Dossin

Library of Congress Control Number: 2001012345

ISBN 978-1-58648-885-7

First Edition

1 3 5 7 9 10 8 6 4 2

CONTENTS

AUTHOR'S NOTE

IN OCTOBER 2009, I delivered this series of lectures in Budapest under the auspices of the Central European University, an international postgraduate institution in the field of humanities and social sciences that I established after the collapse of the Soviet system in 1991.

Lectures One and Two summarize a lifetime of experience and reflection. I lay out in detail the conceptual framework that has guided me in business and philanthropy and apply it to the current turmoil in financial markets. Lectures Three and Four explore what is, for me, newer ground—questions of ethical values and political power and the relationship between the two. The final lecture presents such predictions and prescriptions as my conceptual framework allows.

My goal is ambitious. It is that this conceptual framework should provide the foundation for a better understanding of human affairs. The reader will judge whether I have been successful. I hope that my ideas will be received in the same spirit of critical thinking in which they are offered and not as some sort of dogma.

These lectures and the discussions that followed were

videoconferenced to universities around the world. The recordings are available at the website of the Open Society Institute, www.soros.org/resources/multimedia/sorosceu_20091112.

One of the discussion partners was Fudan University, Shanghai, and another partner was Hong Kong University. I am very pleased about that because I believe China will become increasingly influential in the world, and if my conceptual framework finds a following in China, the world might be a better place. Other partners included Columbia University; the London School of Economics, my *alma mater*; and the Massachusetts Institute of Technology. I was pleased to be able to share my ideas at these distinguished institutions.

I am grateful to those at the Central European University and the Open Society Institute, and to my personal staff who helped make the original presentation and videocasting of these five lectures a success. My thanks also go to my publisher, Peter Osnos, and his colleagues at PublicAffairs. I owe a debt of gratitude to Colin McGinn and Mark Notturno for clarifying certain philosophical points; to John Shattuck, the president of the Central European University; to Anatole Kaletsky, Ivan Krastev, Mark Danner, and Howard Davies for moderating the discussions that followed each lecture; and to Cristovam Buarque and the many others who offered their comments.

GEORGE SOROS

January 2010

New York

LECTURE ONE

THE HUMAN UNCERTAINTY PRINCIPLE

Central European University Lecture Series, October 26–30, 2009

IN THE COURSE OF MY LIFE I have developed a conceptual framework that has helped me to make money as a hedge fund manager and also to spend money as a policy-oriented philanthropist. But the conceptual framework itself is not about money—it is about the relationship between thinking and reality, a subject that has been extensively studied by philosophers from early on. I started developing my philosophy as a student at the London School of Economics in the late 1950s. I took my final exams one year early, so I had a year to fill before I was qualified to receive my degree. I could choose my tutor, and I chose Karl Popper, the Viennese-born philosopher whose book *The Open Society and Its Enemies* had made a profound impression on me.

In his books Popper argued that the empirical truth cannot be known with absolute certainty. Even scientific laws can't be verified beyond a shadow of a doubt: they can only be falsified by testing. One failed test is enough to falsify, but no amount of conforming instances is sufficient to verify. Scientific laws are hypothetical in character and their truth remains open to falsification. Ideologies that claim to be in possession of the ultimate truth are making a false claim; therefore, they can be imposed on society only by compulsion. All such ideologies lead to repression. Popper proposed a more attractive form of social organization: an open society in which people are free to hold divergent opinions and the rule of law allows people with different views and interests to live together in peace. Having lived through both German and Russian occupation here in Hungary, I found the idea of an open society immensely attractive.

While I was reading Popper I was also studying economic theory, and I was struck by the contradiction between Popper's emphasis on imperfect understanding and the theory of perfect competition in economics, which postulated perfect knowledge. This led me to start questioning the assumptions of economic theory. These were the two major theoretical inspirations of my philosophy. There were, of course, many other minor ones.

My philosophy is also deeply rooted in my personal history. The formative experience of my life was the German occupation of Hungary in 1944, when I was not yet fourteen years old. I came from a reasonably well-to-do middle-class background, and I was suddenly confronted with the prospect of being deported and killed just because I was Jewish. Fortunately, my father was well prepared for this far-from-equilibrium experience. He had lived through the Russian Revolution—the formative experience of *his* life. Until then he had been an ambitious young man. When the First World War broke out, he volunteered to serve in the Austro-Hungarian Army. He was captured by the Russians and taken as a prisoner of war to Siberia. Being ambitious, he became the editor of a newspaper produced by the prisoners. It was handwritten and displayed on a plank, and it was called *The Plank*. This made him so popular that he was elected the prisoners' representative.

Then some soldiers escaped from a neighboring camp, and their prisoners' representative was shot in retaliation. My father, instead of waiting for the same thing to happen in his camp, organized a group and led a breakout. His plan was to build a raft and sail down to the ocean, but his knowledge of geography was deficient; he did not know that all the rivers in Siberia flow into the Arctic Sea. They drifted for several weeks before they realized that they were heading for the Arctic, and it took them several more months to make their way back to civilization across the taiga. In the meantime, the Russian Revolution broke out, and they became caught up in it. Only after a variety of adventures did my father manage to find his way back to Hungary; had he remained in the camp, he would have arrived home much sooner.

My father came home a changed man. His experiences during the Russian Revolution profoundly affected him. He lost his ambition and wanted nothing more from life than to enjoy it. He imparted to his children values that were very different from those of the milieu in which we lived. He had no desire to amass wealth or become socially prominent. On the contrary, he worked only as much as was necessary to make ends meet. I remember being sent to his main client to borrow some money before we went on a ski vacation. My father was grouchy for weeks afterward because he had to work to pay it back. Although we were reasonably prosperous, we were not the typical bourgeois family, and we were proud of being different.

In 1944, when the Germans occupied Hungary, my father immediately realized that these were not normal times and that the normal rules didn't apply. He arranged false identities for his family and a number of other people. Those who could, paid; others, he helped for free. Most of them survived. That was his finest hour. Living with a false identity turned out to be a very positive experience for me. With the rest of my family, I was in mortal danger. People perished all around us, but we managed not only to survive but also to help other people. We were on the side of the angels, and we triumphed against overwhelming odds. This made me feel very special. It was high adventure. I had a reliable guide in my father, and I came through unscathed. What more could a fourteen-year-old ask for?

After the euphoric experience of escaping the Nazis, life in Hungary started to lose its luster during the Soviet occupation. I was looking for new challenges, and with my father's help I found my way out of Hungary. When I was seventeen I became a student in London. In my studies, my primary interest was to gain a better understanding of the strange world into which I had been born, but I have to confess, I also harbored some fantasies of becoming an important philosopher. I believed that I had gained insights that set me apart from other people.

Living in London was a big letdown. I was without money, alone, and people were not interested in what I had to say. But I didn't abandon my philosophical ambitions, even when circumstances forced me to make a living in more mundane pursuits. After completing my studies, I had a number of false starts. Finally, I ended up as an arbitrage trader in New York. But in my free time I continued to work on my philosophy.

That is how I came to write my first major essay, "The Burden of Consciousness." It was an attempt to model Popper's framework of open and closed societies. It linked organic society with a traditional mode of thinking, closed society with a dogmatic mode, and open society with a critical mode. What I could not properly resolve was the nature of the relationship between the mode of thinking and the actual state of affairs. That problem continued to preoccupy me, and that is how I came to develop the concept of reflexivity—a concept I shall explore in greater detail a little later.

It so happened that the concept of reflexivity provided me with a new way of looking at financial markets, a better way than the prevailing theory. This gave me an edge, first as a securities analyst and then as a hedge fund manager. I felt as if I were in possession of a major discovery that would enable me to fulfill my fantasy of becoming an important philosopher. At a certain moment when my business career ran into a roadblock, I shifted gears and devoted all my energies to developing my philosophy. But I treasured my discovery so much that I could not part with it. I felt that the concept of reflexivity needed to be explored in depth. As I delved deeper and deeper into the subject, I got lost in the intricacies of my own constructions. One morning I could not understand what I had written the night before. At that point I decided to abandon my philosophical explorations and to focus on making money. It was only many years later, after a successful run as a hedge fund manager, that I returned to my philosophy.

I published my first book, *The Alchemy of Finance*, in 1987. In that book I tried to explain the philosophical underpinnings of my approach to financial markets. The book attracted a certain amount of attention. It has been read by many people in the hedge fund industry and it is taught in business schools, but the philosophical arguments did not make much of an impression. They were largely dismissed as the conceit of a man who has been successful in business and therefore fancies himself as a philosopher.

I myself came to doubt whether I was in possession of a major new insight. After all, I was dealing with a subject that has been explored by philosophers since time immemorial. What grounds did I have for thinking that I had made a new discovery, especially since nobody else seemed to think so? Undoubtedly, the conceptual framework was useful to me personally, but it did not seem to be considered equally valuable by others. I had to accept their judgment. I didn't give up my philosophical interests, but I came to regard them as a personal predilection. I continued to be guided by my conceptual framework in my business and in my philanthropic activities—which came to assume an increasingly important role in my life—and each time I wrote a book I faithfully recited my arguments. This helped me to develop my conceptual framework, but I continued to consider myself a failed philosopher. Once I even gave a lecture with the title "A Failed Philosopher Tries Again."

All this has changed as a result of the financial crisis of 2008. My conceptual framework enabled me both to anticipate the crisis and to deal with it when it finally struck. It has also enabled me to explain and predict events better than most others. This has changed my own evaluation, and that of many others. My philosophy is no longer a personal matter; it deserves to be taken seriously as a possible contribution to our understanding of reality. That is what has prompted me to give this series of lectures. So here it goes.

Today I shall explain the concepts of fallibility and reflexivity in general terms. Tomorrow I shall apply them to the financial markets, and after that, to politics. That will also bring in the concept of open society. In the fourth lecture I shall explore the difference between market values and moral values, and in the fifth I shall offer some predictions and prescriptions for the present moment in history.

I CAN STATE THE CORE IDEA in two relatively simple propositions. One is that in situations that have thinking participants, the participants' view of the world is always partial and distorted. That is the principle of fallibility. The other is that these distorted views can influence the situation to which they relate because false views lead to inappropriate actions. That is the principle of reflexivity. For instance, treating drug addicts as criminals creates criminal behavior. It misconstrues the problem and interferes with the proper treatment of addicts. As another example, declaring that government is bad tends to make for bad government.

Both fallibility and reflexivity are sheer common sense. So when my critics say that I am merely stating the obvious, they are right—but only up to a point. What makes my propositions interesting is that their significance has not been generally appreciated. The concept of reflexivity, in particular, has been studiously avoided and even denied by economic theory. So my conceptual framework deserves to be taken seriously—not because it constitutes a new discovery but because something as commonsensical as reflexivity has been so studiously ignored. Recognizing reflexivity has been sacrificed to the vain pursuit of certainty in human affairs, most notably in economics, and yet uncertainty is the key feature of human affairs. Economic theory is built on the concept of equilibrium, and that concept is in direct contradiction with the concept of reflexivity. As I shall show in the next lecture, the two concepts yield two entirely different interpretations of financial markets.

The concept of fallibility is far less controversial. It is generally recognized that the complexity of the world in which we live exceeds our capacity to comprehend it. I have no great new insights to offer on that subject. The main source of difficulties is that participants are part of the situations they have to deal with. Confronted by a reality of extreme complexity, we are obliged to resort to various methods of simplification: generalizations, dichotomies, metaphors, decision rules, and moral precepts, to mention just a few. These mental constructs take on an existence of their own, further complicating the situation.

The structure of the brain is another source of distortions. Recent advances in brain science have begun to provide some insight into how the brain functions, and they have substantiated David Hume's insight that reason is the slave of passion. The idea of a disembodied intellect or reason is a figment of our imagination. The brain is bombarded by millions of sensory impulses, but consciousness can process only seven or eight subjects concurrently. The impulses need to be condensed, ordered, and interpreted under immense time pressure, and mistakes and distortions can't be avoided. Brain science adds many new details to my original contention that our understanding of the world in which we live is inherently imperfect.

THE CONCEPT OF REFLEXIVITY needs a little more explication. It applies exclusively to situations that have thinking participants. The participants' thinking serves two functions. One is to understand the world in which we live; I call this the *cognitive function*. The other is to change the situation to our advantage. I call this the *participating* or *manipulative function*. The two functions connect thinking and reality in opposite directions. In the cognitive function, reality is supposed to determine the participants' views; the direction of causation is from the world to the mind. By contrast, in the manipulative function, the direction of causation is from the mind to the world—that is to say, the intentions of the participants have an effect on the world. When both functions operate at the same time they can interfere with each other. How? By depriving each function of the independent variable that would be needed to determine the value of the dependent variable: when the independent variable of one function is the dependent variable of the other, neither function has a *genuinely independent variable*.

This means that the cognitive function can't produce enough knowledge to serve as the basis of the participants' decisions. Similarly, the manipulative function can have an impact on the outcome but can't determine it. In other words, the outcome is liable to diverge from the participants' intentions. There is bound to be some slippage between intentions and actions, and further slippage between actions and outcomes. As a result, there is an element of uncertainty in both our understanding of reality and the actual course of events.

To understand the uncertainties associated with reflexivity, we need to probe a little further. If the cognitive function operated in isolation without any interference from the manipulative function, it could produce knowledge. Knowledge is represented by true statements. A statement is true if it corresponds to the facts—that is what the correspondence theory of truth tells us. But if there is interference from the manipulative function, the facts no longer serve as an independent criterion by which the truth of a statement can be judged because the correspondence may have been brought about by the statement changing the facts.

Consider the statement "It is raining." That statement is true or false depending on whether it is, in fact, raining. Now consider the statement "This is a revolutionary moment." That statement is reflexive, and its truth value depends on the impact it makes.

Reflexive statements have some affinity with the paradox of the liar, which involves a self-referential statement. But while self-reference has been extensively analyzed, reflexivity has received much less attention. This is strange because reflexivity has an impact on the real world, while self-reference is purely a linguistic phenomenon.

In the real world, the participants' thinking finds expression not only in statements but also, of course, in various forms of action and behavior. That makes reflexivity a very broad phenomenon that typically takes the form of feedback loops. The participants' views influence the course of events, and the course of events influences the participants' views. The influence is continuous and circular; that is what turns it into a feedback loop. The process may be initiated from either direction; from a change in views or from a change in circumstances.

Reflexive feedback loops have *not* been rigorously analyzed and when I originally encountered them and tried to analyze them, I ran into various complications. The feedback loop is supposed to be a two-way connection between the participants' views and the actual course of events. But what about a two-way connection between the participants' views? And what about a solitary individual asking himself who he is and what he stands for and changing his behavior as a result of his reflections? In trying to resolve these difficulties I got so lost among the categories I created that one morning I couldn't understand what I had written the night before. That's when I gave up philosophy and devoted my efforts to making money.

To avoid the trap I fell into in my earlier exploration of reflexivity, let me propose the following terminology. Let us distinguish between the objective and subjective aspects of reality. Thinking constitutes the subjective aspect, and events constitute the objective aspect. In other words, the subjective aspect covers what takes place in the minds of the participants, and the objective aspect denotes what takes place in external reality. There is only one external reality, but there are many different subjective views. Reflexivity can then connect any two or more aspects of reality, setting up two-way feedback loops between them. In exceptional cases it may even occur within a single aspect of reality, as in the case of a solitary individual reflecting on his own identity. This may be described as *self-reflexivity*. We may then distinguish between two broad categories: reflexive *relations*, which connect the subjective aspects of reality, and reflexive *events*, which involve the objective aspect. When reality has no subjective aspect, there can be no reflexivity.

FEEDBACK LOOPS CAN BE either negative or positive. Negative feedback brings the participants' views and the actual situation closer together; positive feedback drives them further apart. In other words, a negative feedback process is self-correcting. It can go on forever and if there are no significant changes in external reality, it may eventually lead to an equilibrium in which the participants' views come to correspond to the actual state of affairs. That is what is supposed to happen in financial markets. So equilibrium, which is the *central* case in economics, turns out to be an extreme case of negative feedback, a *limiting* case in my conceptual framework.

By contrast, a positive feedback process is self-reinforcing. It cannot go on forever because eventually the participants' views would become so far removed from objective reality that the participants would have to recognize them as unrealistic. Nor can the iterative process occur without any change in the actual state of affairs, because it is the nature of positive feedback to reinforce whatever tendency prevails in the real world. Instead of equilibrium, we are faced with a dynamic disequilibrium, or what may be described as *far-from-equilibrium* situations. Usually in far-from-equilibrium situations the divergence between perceptions and reality produces a climax that sets in motion a positive feedback process in the opposite direction. Such initially self-reinforcing but eventually self-defeating boom-bust processes, or bubbles, are characteristic of financial markets, but they can also be found in other spheres. There, I call them *fertile fallacies*—interpretations of reality that are distorted but produce results that reinforce the distortion.

I REALIZE THAT ALL THIS is very abstract and difficult to follow. Some concrete examples would be helpful. But you will have to bear with me. I want to make a different point, and the fact that abstract arguments are difficult to follow helps me make it. In dealing with abstract concepts like reality or thinking or the relationship between the two, it's easy to get confused and formulate problems the wrong way. So misinterpretations and misconceptions can play a very important role in human affairs. The recent financial crisis can be attributed to a mistaken interpretation of how financial markets work. I shall discuss that in the next lecture. In the third lecture, I shall discuss two fertile fallacies: the Enlightenment fallacy and the postmodern fallacy, and the pervasive influence they have on the way we look at the world. These concrete examples will demonstrate how important misconceptions have been in the course of history. But for the rest of this lecture I shall stay at the lofty heights of abstractions.

I CONTEND THAT SITUATIONS that have thinking participants have a different structure from natural phenomena. The difference lies in the role of thinking. In natural phenomena, thinking plays no *causal* role and serves only a cognitive function. In human affairs thinking is *part of* the subject matter and serves both a cognitive and a manipulative function. The two functions can interfere with each other. The interference does not occur all the time—in everyday activities, like driving a car or painting a house, the two functions actually complement each other—but when it does occur, it introduces an element of uncertainty that is absent from natural phenomena. The uncertainty manifests itself in *both* functions: the participants act on the basis of imperfect understanding, and the results of their actions will not correspond to their expectations. That is a key feature of human affairs.

By contrast, in the case of natural phenomena, events unfold irrespective of the views held by the observers. The outside observer is engaged only in the cognitive function and the phenomena provide a reliable criterion by which the truth of the observers' theories can be judged. So the outside observer can obtain knowledge. Based on that knowledge, nature can be successfully manipulated. There is a natural separation between the cognitive and manipulative functions. Due to their separation, both functions can serve their purpose better than in the human sphere.

At this point I need to emphasize that reflexivity is not the only source of uncertainty in human affairs. Yes, reflexivity does introduce an element of uncertainty into both the participants' views and the actual course of events, but other factors may also have the same effect. For instance, the fact that participants cannot know what the other participants know is something quite different from reflexivity, yet it is a source of uncertainty in human affairs. The fact that different participants have different interests, some of which may be in conflict with each other, is another source of uncertainty. Moreover, each participant may be guided by a multiplicity of values that may not be self-consistent, as Isaiah Berlin pointed out. The uncertainties created by these factors are likely to be even more extensive than those generated by reflexivity. I will lump them all together and speak of the *human uncertainty principle*, which is an even broader concept than reflexivity.

The human uncertainty principle is much more specific and stringent than the subjective skepticism that pervades Cartesian philosophy. It gives us objective reasons to believe that our perceptions and expectations are—or at least may be—wrong.

ALTHOUGH THE PRIMARY effects of human uncertainty fall on the participants, it has far-reaching implications for the social sciences. I can explicate them best by invoking Popper's theory of scientific method. It is a beautifully simple and elegant scheme. It consists of three elements and three operations. The three elements are scientific laws and the initial and final conditions to which those laws apply. The three operations are prediction, explanation, and testing. When the scientific laws are combined with initial conditions, they provide predictions. When they are combined with final conditions, they provide explanations. In this sense, predictions and explanations are symmetrical and reversible. That leaves testing, in which predictions derived from scientific laws are compared with actual results.

According to Popper, scientific laws are hypothetical in character; they cannot be verified, but they can be falsified by testing. The key to the success of scientific method is that it can test generalizations of universal validity with the help of singular observations. One failed test is sufficient to falsify a theory, but no amount of confirming instances is sufficient to verify.

This is a brilliant solution to the otherwise intractable problem of how science can be both empirical and rational. According to Popper it is empirical because we *test* our theories by observing whether the predictions we derive from them are true, and it is rational because we use deductive logic in doing so. Popper dispenses with inductive logic and relies instead on testing. Generalizations that cannot be falsified do not qualify as scientific. Popper emphasizes the central role that testing plays in scientific method and establishes a strong case for critical thinking by asserting that scientific laws are only provisionally valid and remain open to reexamination. Thus the three salient features of Popper's scheme are the symmetry between prediction and explanation, the asymmetry between verification and falsification, and the central role of testing. Testing allows science to grow, improve, and innovate.

Popper's scheme works well for the study of natural phenomena, but the human uncertainty principle throws a monkey wrench into the supreme simplicity and elegance of Popper's scheme. The symmetry between prediction and explanation is destroyed because of the element of uncertainty in predictions, and the central role of testing is endangered. Should the initial and final conditions include or exclude the participant's thinking? The question is important because testing requires replicating those conditions. If the participants' thinking is included, it is difficult to observe what the initial and final conditions are because the participants' views can only be inferred from their statements or actions. If it is excluded, the initial and final conditions do not constitute singular observations because the same objective conditions may be associated with very different views held by the participants. In either case, generalizations cannot be properly tested. These difficulties do not preclude social scientists from producing worthwhile generalizations, but they are unlikely to meet the requirements of Popper's scheme, nor can they match the predictive power of the laws of physics.

Social scientists have found this conclusion hard to accept. Economists in particular suffer from what Sigmund Freud might call "physics envy."

THERE HAVE BEEN MANY attempts to eliminate the difficulties connected with the human uncertainty principle by inventing or postulating some kind of fixed relationship between the participants' thinking and the actual state of affairs. Karl Marx asserted that the ideological superstructure was determined by the material conditions of production, and Freud maintained that people's behavior was determined by drives and complexes of which they were not even conscious. Both claimed scientific status for their theories, although, as Popper pointed out, they cannot be falsified by testing.

But by far the most impressive attempt has been mounted by

economic theory. It started out by assuming perfect knowledge, and when that assumption turned out to be untenable it went through ever-increasing contortions to maintain the fiction of rational behavior. Economics ended up with the theory of rational expectations, which maintains that there is a single optimum view of the future, that which corresponds to it, and eventually all the market participants will converge around that view. This postulate is absurd, but it is needed in order to allow economic theory to model itself on Newtonian physics.

Interestingly, both Karl Popper and Friedrich Hayek recognized, in their famous exchange in the pages of *Economica*, that the social sciences cannot produce results comparable to physics. Hayek inveighed against the mechanical and uncritical application of the quantitative methods of natural science. He called it "scientism." And Popper wrote "The Poverty of Historicism," in which he argued that history is not determined by universally valid scientific laws.

Nevertheless, Popper proclaimed what he called the "doctrine of the unity of method," by which he meant that both natural and social sciences should be judged by the same criteria. And Hayek, of course, became an apostle of the Chicago school of economics, where market fundamentalism originated. But as I see it, the implication of the human uncertainty principle is that the subject matter of the natural and social sciences is fundamentally different; therefore they need to develop different methods and they have to be held to different standards. Economic theory should not be expected to produce universally valid laws that can be used reversibly to explain and predict events in history. I contend that the slavish imitation of natural science inevitably leads to the distortion of human and social phenomena. What social science can attain by imitating natural science falls short of what is attainable in physics.

I AM SOMEWHAT TROUBLED about drawing too sharp a distinction between natural and social science. Such dichotomies are usually not found in reality; they are introduced by us, in our efforts to make some sense out of an otherwise confusing reality. Indeed, while a sharp distinction between physics and social sciences seems justified, there are other sciences, such as biology and the study of animal societies that occupy intermediate positions.

Nevertheless, I have to abandon my reservations and recognize a dichotomy between the natural and social sciences because the social sciences encounter a second difficulty, in addition to the human uncertainty principle, from which the natural sciences are exempt. And that is that social theories themselves are reflexive.

Werner Heisenberg's discovery of the uncertainty principle in physics did not alter the behavior of quantum particles one iota, but social theories—whether Marxism, market fundamentalism, or the theory of reflexivity—can affect the subject matter to which it refers. Scientific method is supposed to be devoted to the pursuit of truth.

Heisenberg's uncertainty principle does not interfere with that postulate, but the reflexivity of social theories does. Why should social science confine itself to passively studying social phenomena when it can be used to actively change the state of affairs? As I remarked in *The Alchemy of Finance*, the alchemists made a mistake in trying to change the nature of base metals by incantation. Instead, they should have focused their attention on the financial markets, where they could have succeeded.

How could social science be protected against this interference? I propose a simple remedy: recognize a dichotomy between the natural and social sciences. This will ensure that social theories will be judged on their merits and not by a false analogy with natural science. I propose this as a convention for the protection of scientific method, not as a demotion or devaluation of social science. The convention sets no limits on what social science may be able to accomplish. On the contrary, by liberating social science from the slavish imitation of natural science and protecting it from being judged by the wrong standards, it should open up new vistas. It is in this spirit that I shall put forward my interpretation of financial markets tomorrow.

I apologize for dwelling so long in the rarefied realm of abstractions. I promise to come down to earth in my next lecture.

Thank you.

LECTURE TWO

FINANCIAL MARKETS

Central European University Lecture Series,

October 26–30, 2009

IN THIS LECTURE I'll apply the concepts introduced in the first lecture—fallibility, reflexivity, and the human uncertainty principle—to the financial markets. Please brace yourselves, because I'll pack the experience of a lifetime into this one lecture.

Financial markets provide an excellent laboratory for testing the ideas I put forward in an abstract form in the previous lecture. The course of events is easier to observe than in most other areas. Many of the facts take a quantitative form, and the data are well recorded and well preserved. The opportunity for testing occurs because my interpretation of financial markets directly contradicts the efficient market hypothesis, which has been the prevailing theory about financial markets. The efficient market hypothesis claims that markets tend toward equilibrium; that deviations occur in a random fashion and can be attributed to extraneous shocks. If that theory is valid, mine is false—and vice versa.

LET ME STATE THE TWO cardinal principles of my conceptual framework as it applies to the financial markets. First, market prices always distort the underlying fundamentals. The degree of distortion may range from the negligible to the significant. This is in direct contradiction to the efficient market hypothesis, which maintains that market prices accurately reflect all the available information.

Second, instead of playing a purely passive role in reflecting an underlying reality, financial markets also have an active role: they can *affect* the so-called fundamentals they are supposed to reflect. That is the point that behavioral economics is missing. That discipline focuses on only half of a reflexive process: the mispricing of financial assets; it does not concern itself with the effect the mispricing has on the fundamentals.

There are various pathways by which the mispricing of financial assets can affect the so-called fundamentals. The most widely traveled are those that involve the use of leverage—both debt and equity leveraging. The various feedback loops may give the impression that markets are often right, but the mechanism at work is very different from the one proposed by the prevailing paradigm. I claim that financial markets have ways of altering the fundamentals and that the resulting alterations may bring about a closer correspondence between market prices and the underlying fundamentals. Contrast that with the efficient market hypothesis, which claims that markets always accurately reflect reality and automatically tend toward equilibrium.

My two propositions focus attention on the reflexive feedback loops that characterize financial markets. I described the two kinds of feedback, negative and positive, in the first lecture. Again, negative feedback is self-correcting, and positive feedback is self-reinforcing. Thus, negative feedback sets up a tendency toward equilibrium, but positive feedback produces dynamic disequilibrium. Positive feedback loops are more interesting because they can cause big moves, both in market prices and in the underlying fundamentals. A positive feedback process that runs its full course is initially self-reinforcing in one direction, but eventually it is liable to reach a climax or reversal point, after which it becomes self-reinforcing in the opposite direction. But positive feedback processes do not necessarily run their full course; they may be aborted at any time by negative feedback.

I HAVE DEVELOPED A THEORY about boom-bust processes, or bubbles, along these lines. Every bubble has two components: an underlying trend that prevails in reality and a misconception relating to that trend. A boom-bust process is set in motion when a trend and a misconception positively reinforce each other. The process is liable to be tested by negative feedback along the way. If the trend is strong enough to survive the test, both the trend and the misconception will be further reinforced. Eventually, market expectations become so far removed from reality that people are forced to recognize that a misconception is involved. A twilight period ensues during which doubts grow and more people loose faith, but the prevailing trend is sustained by inertia. As Chuck Prince, former head of Citigroup said: "As long as the music is playing, you've got to get up and dance. We're still dancing." Eventually a point is reached when the trend is reversed; it then becomes self-reinforcing in the opposite direction.

Let me go back to the example I used when I originally proposed my theory in 1987: the conglomerate boom of the late 1960s. The underlying trend is represented by earnings per share, the expectations relating to that trend by stock prices. Conglomerates improved their earnings per share by acquiring other companies. Inflated expectations allowed them to improve their earnings performance, but eventually reality could not keep up with expectations. After a twilight period the price trend was reversed. All the problems that had been swept under the carpet surfaced, and earnings collapsed. As the president of one of the conglomerates, Ogden Corporation, told me at the time: I have no audience to play to.

The chart below is a model of the conglomerate bubble. The charts of actual conglomerates like Ogden Corporation closely resemble this chart. Bubbles that conform to this pattern go through distinct stages: (1) inception; (2) a period of acceleration, (3) interrupted and reinforced by successful tests; (4) a twilight period; (5) and the reversal point or climax, (6) followed by acceleration on the downside (7) culminating in a financial crisis.

The length and strength of each stage is unpredictable, but there is an internal logic to the sequence of stages. So the sequence is predictable, but even that can be terminated by government

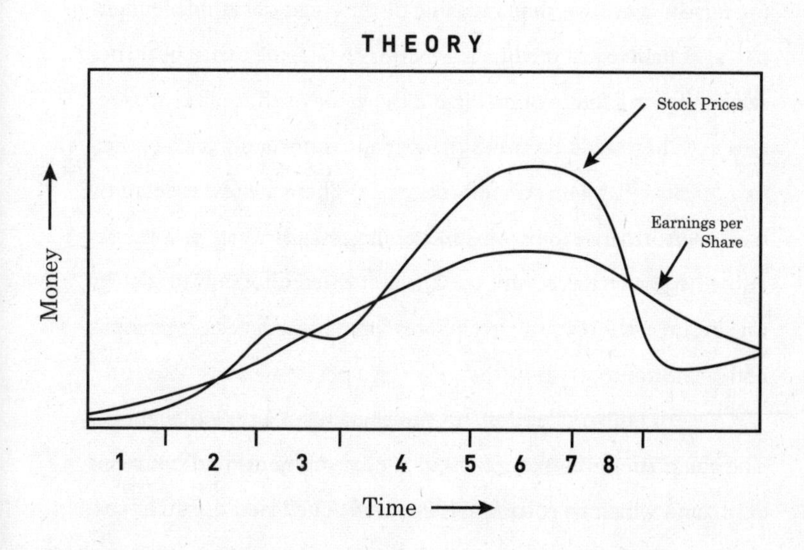

intervention or some other form of negative feedback. In the case of the conglomerate boom, it was the defeat of Leasco Systems and Research Corporation in its attempt to acquire Manufacturer Hanover Trust Company that constituted the climax, or reversal point.

Typically, bubbles have an asymmetric shape. The boom is long and drawn out; slow to start, it accelerates gradually until it flattens out during the twilight period. The bust is short and steep because it is reinforced by the forced liquidation of unsound positions. Disillusionment turns into panic, reaching its climax in a financial crisis.

The simplest case is a real estate boom. The trend that precipitates it is that credit becomes cheaper and more easily available; the misconception is that the value of the collateral is independent of the availability of credit. As a matter of fact, the relationship between the availability of credit and the value of the collateral is reflexive. When credit becomes cheaper and more easily available, activity picks up and real estate values rise. There are fewer defaults, credit performance improves, and lending standards are relaxed. So at the height of the boom, the amount of credit involved is at its maximum and a reversal precipitates forced liquidation, depressing real estate values.

Yet, the misconception continues to recur in various guises. The international banking crisis of 1982 revolved around sovereign debt, with which no collateral is involved. The creditworthiness of the sovereign borrowers was measured by various debt ratios, such as debt to GDP or debt service to exports. These ratios were considered objective criteria, but in fact they were reflexive. When the recycling of petro-dollars in the 1970s increased the flow of credit to countries like Brazil, their debt ratios improved, encouraging further inflows and starting a bubble. Shortly after Paul Volcker raised interest rates in the U.S. to arrest inflation, the bubble burst.

Not all bubbles involve the extension of credit; some are based on equity leveraging. The best examples are the conglomerate boom of the late 1960s and the Internet bubble of the late 1990s. When Alan Greenspan spoke about irrational exuberance in 1996, he misrepresented bubbles. When I see a bubble forming I rush in to buy, adding fuel to the fire. That is not irrational. And that is why we need regulators to counteract the market when a bubble is threatening to grow too big; we cannot rely on market participants, however well informed and rational they are.

Bubbles are not the only form in which reflexivity manifests itself. They are just the most dramatic and the most directly opposed to the efficient market hypothesis; so they do deserve special attention. But reflexivity can take many other forms. In currency markets, for instance, the upside and downside are symmetrical so that there is no sign of an asymmetry between boom and bust. But there is no sign of equilibrium either. Freely floating exchange rates tend to move in large, multi-year waves.

The most important and most interesting reflexive interaction takes place between the financial authorities and financial markets. Because markets do not tend toward equilibrium, they are prone to produce periodic crises. Financial crises lead to regulatory reforms. That is how central banking and the regulation of financial markets have evolved. Financial authorities and market participants alike act on the basis of imperfect understanding, and that makes the interaction between them reflexive.

While bubbles only occur intermittently, the interplay between authorities and markets is an ongoing process. Misunderstandings by either side usually stay within reasonable bounds because market reactions provide useful feedback to the authorities, allowing them to correct their mistakes. But occasionally the mistakes prove to be self-validating, setting in motion vicious or virtuous circles. Such feedback loops resemble bubbles in the sense that they are initially self-reinforcing but eventually self-defeating. Indeed, the intervention of the authorities to deal with periodic financial crises played a crucial role in the development of a "superbubble" that burst in 2007–2008.

It is important to realize that not all price distortions are due to reflexivity. Market participants cannot possibly base their decisions on knowledge—they have to anticipate the future, and the future is contingent on decisions that people have not yet made. What those decisions are going to be and what effect they will have cannot be accurately anticipated. Nevertheless, people are forced to make decisions. To guess correctly, people would have to know the decisions of all of the other participants and their consequences, but that is impossible.

Rational expectations theory sought to circumvent this impossibility by postulating that there is a single correct set of expectations and people's views will converge around it. That postulate has no resemblance to reality, but it is the basis of financial economics as it is currently taught in universities. In practice, participants are obliged to make their decisions in conditions of uncertainty. Their decisions are bound to be tentative and biased. That is the generic cause of price distortions.

Occasionally, the price distortions set in motion a boom-bust process. More often, they are corrected by negative feedback. In these cases market fluctuations have a random character. I compare them to the waves sloshing around in a swimming pool as opposed to tidal waves. Obviously, the latter are more significant but the former are more ubiquitous. The two kinds of price distortions intermingle so that in reality boom-bust processes rarely follow the exact course of my model. Bubbles that follow the pattern I described in my model occur only on those rare occasions when they are so powerful that they overshadow all the other processes going on at the same time.

IT WILL BE USEFUL TO DISTINGUISH between near-equilibrium conditions, which are characterized by random fluctuations, and far-from-equilibrium situations, in which a bubble predominates. Near-equilibrium is characterized by humdrum, everyday events that are repetitive and lend themselves to statistical generalizations. Far-from-equilibrium conditions give rise to unique, historic events in which outcomes are generally uncertain but have the capacity to disrupt the statistical generalizations based on everyday events.

The rules that can guide decisions in near equilibrium conditions do not apply in far-from-equilibrium situations. The recent financial crisis is a case in point. All the risk management tools and synthetic financial products that were based on the assumption that price deviations from a putative equilibrium occur in a random fashion broke down, and people who relied on mathematical models that had served them well in near-equilibrium conditions got badly hurt.

I have gained some new insights into far-from-equilibrium conditions during the recent financial crisis. As a participant I had to act under immense time pressure, and I could not gather all of the information that would have been available—and the same applied to the regulatory authorities in charge. That is how far-from-equilibrium situations can spin out of control.

This situation is not confined to financial markets. I experienced it, for instance, during the collapse of the Soviet Union. The fact that the participants' thinking is time-bound instead of timeless is left out of the account by rational expectations theory.

I was aware of the uncertainty associated with reflexivity, but even I was taken by surprise by the extent of the uncertainty in 2008. It cost me dearly. I got the general direction of the markets right, but I did not allow for the volatility. As a consequence, I took on positions that were too big to withstand the swings caused by volatility, and several times I was forced to reduce my positions at the wrong time in order to limit my risk. I would have done better if I had taken smaller positions and stuck with them. I learned the hard way that the range of uncertainty is also uncertain and at times can become practically infinite.

Uncertainty finds expression in volatility. Increased volatility requires a reduction in risk exposure. This leads to what John Maynard Keynes called "increased liquidity preference." This is an additional factor in the forced liquidation of positions that characterizes financial crises. When the crisis abates and the range of uncertainty is reduced, it leads to an almost automatic rebound in the stock market as the liquidity preference stops rising and eventually falls. That is another lesson I have learned recently.

I need to point out that I introduced the distinction between near- and far-from-equilibrium conditions in order to make some sense out of a confusing reality, and it does not accurately describe reality. Reality is always more complicated than the dichotomies we introduce into it. The recent crisis is comparable to a hundred-year storm. We have had a number of crises leading up to it. These are comparable to five- or ten-year storms. Regulators who had successfully dealt with the smaller storms were less successful when they applied the same methods to the hundred-year storm.

THESE GENERAL REMARKS prepare the ground for a specific hypothesis to explain the recent financial crisis. It is not derived from my theory of bubbles by deductive logic. Nevertheless, the two of them stand or fall together.

So here it goes. I contend that the puncturing of the subprime bubble in 2007 set off the explosion of a super-bubble, much as an ordinary bomb sets off a nuclear explosion. The housing bubble in the United States was the most common kind, distinguished only by the widespread use of collateralized debt obligations and other synthetic instruments. Behind this ordinary bubble there was a much larger super-bubble growing over a longer period of time that was much more peculiar.

The prevailing trend in this super-bubble was the ever increasing use of credit and leverage. The prevailing misconception was the belief that financial markets are self-correcting and should be left to their own devices. President Reagan called it the "magic of the marketplace," and I call it market fundamentalism. It became the dominant creed in the 1980s, when Ronald Reagan was president of the United States and Margaret Thatcher was prime minister of the United Kingdom.

What made the super-bubble so peculiar was the role that financial crises played in making it grow. Since the belief that markets could be safely left to their own devices was false, the super-bubble gave rise to a series of financial crises. The first and most serious one was the international banking crisis of 1982. This was followed by many other crises, the most notable being the portfolio insurance debacle of October 1987, the savings and loan crisis that unfolded in various episodes between 1989 and 1994, the emerging market crisis of 1997–1998, and the bursting of the Internet bubble in 2000. Each time a financial crisis occurred, the authorities intervened, merged away or otherwise took care of the failing financial institutions, and applied monetary and fiscal stimuli to protect the economy. These measures reinforced the prevailing trend of ever increasing credit and leverage, but as long as they worked, they also reinforced the prevailing misconception that markets can be safely left to their own devices. It was a misconception because it was the intervention of the authorities that saved the system; nevertheless these crises served as successful tests of a false belief, and as such, they inflated the super-bubble even further.

Eventually the credit expansion became unsustainable and the super-bubble exploded. The collapse of the subprime mortgage market in 2007 led to the collapse of one market after another in quick succession because they were all interconnected, the firewalls having been removed by deregulation. And that is what distinguishes the most recent financial crisis from all those that preceded it. Those functioned as successful tests that reinforced the process; the subprime crisis of 2007 constituted the turning point. The collapse then reached its climax with the bankruptcy of Lehman Brothers on September 15, 2008, which precipitated the large-scale intervention of the financial authorities.

It is characteristic of my boom-bust model that it cannot predict whether a test will be successful or not. This holds for ordinary bubbles as well as the super-bubble. I thought that the emerging market crisis of 1997–1998 would constitute the turning point of the super-bubble, but I was wrong. The authorities managed to save the system and the super-bubble continued growing. That made the bust that eventually came in 2007–2008 all the more devastating.

After the bankruptcy of Lehman Brothers financial markets had to be put on artificial life support. This was a shock not only for the financial sector but also for the real economy. International trade was particularly badly hit. But the artificial life support worked, and financial markets stabilized. The economy gradually revived. A year later, the whole episode feels like a bad dream and people would like to forget it. There is a widespread desire to treat the crisis as just another crisis and return to business as usual. But reality is unlikely to oblige. The system is actually broken and needs to be fixed.

MY ANALYSIS OFFERS some worthwhile clues to the kind of regulatory reform that is needed. First and foremost, since markets are bubble-prone, the financial authorities have to accept responsibility for preventing bubbles from growing too big. Alan Greenspan and others have expressly refused to accept that responsibility. If markets can't recognize bubbles, Greenspan argued, neither can regulators—and he was right. Nevertheless, the financial authorities have to accept the assignment, knowing full well that they will not be able to meet it without making mistakes. They will, however, have the benefit of receiving feedback from the markets, which will tell them whether they have done too much or too little. They can then correct their mistakes.

Second, in order to control asset bubbles it is not enough to control the money supply; you must also control the availability of credit. This cannot be done by using only monetary tools; you must also use credit controls. The best-known tools are margin requirements and minimum capital requirements. Currently they are fixed irrespective of the market's mood, because markets are not supposed to have moods. Yet they do, and the financial authorities need to *vary* margin and minimum capital requirements in order to control asset bubbles.

Regulators may also have to invent new tools or revive others that have fallen into disuse. For instance, in my early days in finance, many years ago, central banks used to instruct commercial banks to limit their lending to a particular sector of the economy, such as real estate or consumer loans, because they felt that the sector was overheating. Market fundamentalists consider that to be crass interference with the market mechanism, but they are wrong. When our central banks used to do it we had no financial crises to speak of. The Chinese authorities do it today, and they have much better control over their banking system. The deposits that Chinese commercial banks have to maintain at the People's Bank of China were increased seventeen times during the boom, and when the authorities reversed course the banks obeyed them with alacrity.

Or consider the Internet boom. Alan Greenspan recognized it quite early when he spoke about irrational exuberance in 1996. But apart from his famous speech, he did nothing to avert it. He felt that reducing the money supply would have been too blunt an instrument to use, and he was right. But he could have asked the Securities and Exchange Commission to put a freeze on new share issues since the Internet boom was fueled by equity leveraging. He did not, because that would have violated his market fundamentalist beliefs. That was wrong.

Third, since markets are potentially unstable, there are systemic risks in addition to the risks affecting individual market participants. Participants may ignore these systemic risks in the belief that they can always dispose of their positions, but regulators cannot ignore them because if too many participants are on the same side, positions cannot be liquidated without causing a discontinuity or a collapse. They have to monitor the positions of participants in order to detect potential imbalances. That means that the positions of all major market participants, including hedge funds and sovereign wealth funds, need to be monitored. Certain derivatives, such as credit default swaps and knockout options, are particularly prone to create hidden imbalances; therefore, they must be regulated and, if appropriate, restricted or forbidden. The issuing of synthetic securities needs to be subject to regulatory approval, just as the issuing of ordinary securities is.

Fourth, we must recognize that financial markets evolve in a one-directional, nonreversible manner. The financial authorities, in carrying out their duty of preventing the system from collapsing, have extended an implicit guarantee to all institutions that are "too big to fail." Now they cannot credibly withdraw as long as that guarantees there are institutions that are too big to fail. Therefore, they must impose regulations that will ensure that the guarantee will not be invoked. Too-big-to-fail banks must use less leverage and accept various restrictions on how they invest the depositors' money. Deposits should not be used to finance proprietary trading. But regulators have to go even further. They must regulate the compensation packages of proprietary traders to ensure that risks and rewards are properly aligned. This may push proprietary traders out of banks into hedge funds where they properly belong.

Just as oil tankers are compartmentalized in order to keep them stable, there ought to be firewalls between different markets. It is probably impractical to separate investment banking from commercial banking as the Glass-Steagall Act of 1933 did. But there have to be internal compartments keeping proprietary trading in various markets separate from each other. Some banks that have come to occupy quasi-monopolistic positions may have to be broken up.

Finally, the drafters of the Basel Accords made a mistake when they gave securities held by banks substantially lower risk ratings than regular loans: they ignored the systemic risks attached to concentrated positions in securities. This was an important factor aggravating the crisis. It has to be corrected by raising the risk ratings of securities held by banks, which will probably discourage the securitization of loans.

ALL OF THESE MEASURES will reduce the profitability and leverage of banks. This raises an interesting question about timing. This is not the right time to enact permanent reforms. The financial system and the economy are very far from equilibrium, and they cannot be brought back to near-equilibrium conditions by a straightforward corrective move, just as when a car is skidding you must first turn the wheel in the direction of the skid before you right the car. What needed to be done in the short term was almost exactly the opposite of what is needed in the long term. First, the credit that evaporated had to be replaced by using the only source that has remained credible—namely, the state. That meant increasing the national debt and extending the monetary base. As the economy stabilizes, the monetary base must be shrunk as fast as credit revives—otherwise, deflation will be replaced by the specter of inflation.

We are still in the first phase of this delicate maneuver. The banks are in the process of earning their way out of a hole. To reduce their profitability now would be directly counterproductive. Regulatory reform has to await the second phase, when the money supply needs to be brought under control; and it needs to be carefully phased in so as not to disrupt recovery. But we cannot afford to forget about it.

YOU HAVE SEEN THAT my interpretation of financial markets—call it the theory of reflexivity—is very different from the efficient market hypothesis. Strictly speaking, neither theory is falsifiable by Popper's standards. I predicted the bursting of the super-bubble in 1998. I was wrong then; am I right now? And some proponents of the efficient market hypothesis are still defending it in the face of all the evidence.

Still, there is a widespread feeling that we need a new paradigm, and I contend that my theory provides a better explanation than the available alternatives. Behavioral economics, which is gaining increased recognition, deals with only half of reflexivity: the misinterpretations of reality; it does not study the pathways by which mispricing can change the fundamentals.

I realize that my theory of financial markets is still very rudimentary and needs a lot more development. Obviously, I cannot fully develop it on my own. So I may have been premature in putting forward my theory as the new paradigm. But the efficient market hypothesis has been conclusively disproved and a new interpretation of financial markets is urgently needed. Even more than that, the entire edifice of global financial markets, which was erected on the false premise that markets can be left to their own devices, has to be rebuilt from the ground up.

THIS CONCLUDES THE lecture, but I also want to make an announcement.

I have decided to sponsor an Institute for New Economic Thinking—INET for short. It will be a major institution, fostering research, workshops, and curricula that will develop an alternative to the prevailing paradigm. I have committed $50 million over ten years, and I hope others will join me to bring the budget up to $10 million a year or more.

I hope reflexivity will be one of the concepts that will be explored, but clearly it should not be the only concept. I recognize a potential conflict between being a protagonist and a financial sponsor at the same time. To protect against it, I want to erect a Chinese wall between me and the Institute. To this end, I will extend my financial support through Central European University, and I will not personally participate in the governance of INET. The jury that selects grantees will be expressly instructed to encourage other alternatives besides the theory of reflexivity.

The plan is to launch INET at a workshop on the lessons of the financial crisis at King's College, Cambridge, on April 10 and 11, 2010. And I hope that the new economic thinking will find a home here at the Central European University.

Thank you.

LECTURE THREE

OPEN SOCIETY

Central European University Lecture Series,

October 26–30, 2009

TODAY I SHALL INTRODUCE the third pillar of my conceptual framework, namely, open society. In the previous lectures I was summarizing the conclusions of a lifetime of study and experimentation. Here I will be breaking new ground because my views on open society have changed over time and they are still evolving. As a result, the next two lectures will be much more exploratory in character.

The connection between open society and reflexivity is far from obvious. On a personal level they are closely connected. As you will recall, I was studying economic theory and at the same time I was reading Karl Popper's *Open Society and Its Enemies*. It was Popper's insistence on our inherent fallibility that led me to question the basic assumptions of economic theory and develop the concept of reflexivity.

But on a conceptual level the connection is only indirect. It is the first pillar, fallibility, that connects the other two. Fallibility in this context means not only that our view of the world is always incomplete and distorted but also that in our effort to simplify an extremely complex reality, we often misconstrue it. And our misconceptions play an important role in shaping the course of history.

If there is anything really original in my thinking it is this emphasis on misconceptions. It provides a strong argument in favor of critical thinking and open society.

POPPER DID NOT GIVE an exact definition of open society because he considered exact definitions incompatible with our imperfect understanding. He preferred to approach things from the opposite direction, by first describing them and then giving them a label. The form of social organization he named "open society" bore a close resemblance to democracy.

The net effect of his approach was to justify democracy by an epistemological argument. Since perfect knowledge is beyond the scope of the human intellect, a society characterized by the freedom of speech and thought and free elections is preferable to a society that imposes its ideology by force. Having been exposed to Nazi persecution and Communist oppression, I found this argument very persuasive.

Popper's philosophy made me more sensitive to the role of misconceptions in financial markets, and the concept of reflexivity allowed me to develop my theory of bubbles. This gave me a leg up as a market participant.

After a successful run as a hedge fund manager I went through a kind of midlife crisis. I was approaching fifty. My hedge fund had grown to $100 million, of which about $40 million belonged to me personally. I felt that I had made more than enough money for myself and my family, and running a hedge fund was extremely stressful and depleting. What would make it worthwhile to continue?

I thought long and hard and finally I decided to set up a foundation devoted to the promotion of open society. I defined its mission as opening up closed societies, correcting the deficiencies of open societies, and promoting a critical mode of thinking.

As time went by, I became increasingly involved in philanthropy. I established a foundation in Hungary in 1984 when it was still under Communist rule, in China in 1986, and in Poland and the Soviet Union in 1987. And as the Soviet Union and Yugoslavia disintegrated, I set up a network of foundations that covered almost the entire former Communist world.

In this way I acquired some practical experience in building open societies. I learned a lot. I discovered things that I should have known in the first place—for instance, the disintegration of closed societies does not necessarily lead to the birth of open societies; it may just result in a continuing disintegration until a new regime emerges that bears more resemblance to the regime that had collapsed than to an open society.

THE EVENT THAT FORCED me to thoroughly reconsider the concept of open society was the reelection of George W. Bush in the United States in 2004. Here was the oldest and most successful democracy in the world violating the principles for which it was supposed to stand by engaging in human rights violations in the name of fighting a war on terror and invading Iraq on false pretenses. Yet, he was reelected. How was that possible? I had to ask myself: what was wrong with America? I wrote a couple of books trying to answer that question. I blamed the Bush administration for misleading the people and I blamed the people for allowing the Bush administration to mislead them.

As I probed deeper, I started to question my own conceptual framework. I discovered a flaw in the concept of open society. Popper was mainly concerned with the problems of understanding of reality. He put forward an epistemological rather than a political argument in favor of open society. He argued that "only democracy provides an institutional framework that permits reform without violence, and so the use of reason in politics matters."

But his approach was based on a hidden assumption, namely, that the main purpose of thinking is to gain a better understanding of reality. And that was not necessarily the case. The manipulative function could take precedence over the cognitive function. Indeed, in a democracy, the primary objective of politicians is to get elected and then stay in power.

This rather obvious insight raised some additional questions about the concept of open society. How could Popper take it for granted that free political discourse is aimed at understanding reality? And even more intriguingly, how could I, who gave the manipulative function pride of place in the concept of reflexivity, follow him so blindly?

BOTH QUESTIONS LED ME to the same conclusion: our view of the world is deeply rooted in an intellectual tradition that either ignores the manipulative function or treats it as subservient to the cognitive function.

It is easy to see how this view of the world became so ingrained. The aim of the cognitive function is to produce knowledge. Knowledge is expressed by statements that correspond to the facts. To establish correspondence, statements and facts have to be separate and distinct. Hence, the pursuit of knowledge requires that thoughts should be distinguished from their subject matter. This requirement led philosophers, whose primary preoccupation is with thinking, to the belief that reason and reality are separate. This dualism had its roots in Greek philosophy, and it came to dominate our view of the world during the Enlightenment.

The philosophers of the Enlightenment put their faith in reason. Reason was supposed to work like a searchlight, illuminating a reality that lay there, passively awaiting discovery. The active role that reason can play in shaping reality was largely left out of the account. In other words, the Enlightenment failed to recognize reflexivity. This resulted in a distorted view of reality, but one that was appropriate to the age when it was formulated.

At the time of the Enlightenment humankind had as yet relatively little knowledge of or control over the forces of nature, and scientific method held out infinite promise. It was appropriate to think of reality as something out there, something waiting passively to be discovered, and to think of reason as actively engaged in exploring it. After all, at that time not even the earth had been fully explored. Gathering facts and establishing relationships among them was richly rewarding. Knowledge was being acquired in so many different ways and from so many different directions that the possibilities seemed unlimited. Reason was sweeping away centuries of traditional relationships and religious dogma and generating a triumphant sense of progress.

The difficulties that reflexivity poses to a proper understanding of human affairs went largely unnoticed. The leaders of the

French Revolution believed that reason could help reconstruct society from the ground up, but their faith in reason was excessive. Society failed to follow the dictates of reason, and the euphoria of 1789 deteriorated into the terror of 1794.

The Enlightenment misinterpreted reality by introducing a dichotomy between thinking and reality that would enable reason to attain perfect knowledge. The dichotomy was not inherent in the subject matter but introduced by the philosophers of the Enlightenment in their attempt to make sense of reality.

The mistake made by the Enlightenment philosophers has been given a name; postmodernists call it the "Enlightenment fallacy." I shall adopt that term here, but I want to make it clear that I am talking about a fertile fallacy, one that contains a valuable kernel of truth.

Let me explain more precisely what I mean by "fertile fallacy." We are capable of acquiring knowledge, but we can never have enough knowledge to allow us to base all our decisions on knowledge. It follows that if a piece of knowledge has proved useful, we are liable to overexploit it and extend it to areas where it no longer applies, so that it becomes a fallacy.

That is what happened to the Enlightenment. The dichotomy between reason and reality worked very well for the study of natural phenomena, but it was misleading in the study of human affairs. Fertile fallacies are, in other branches of history, the equivalent of bubbles in financial markets.

The Enlightenment fallacy is deeply rooted in our view of the world. It led Popper to proclaim that the same standards and criteria apply in both the natural and social sciences, and it led economic theory to model itself on Newtonian physics. Neither Popper's elegant model of scientific method nor economic theory recognized reflexivity. What is worse, even I, who discovered—or invented—reflexivity in financial markets, failed to recognize that Popper's concept of open society was based on the hidden assumption that the cognitive function takes precedence over the manipulative function—that we are pursuing the truth and not simply trying to manipulate people into believing what we want them to believe.

The Enlightenment fallacy is also at the root of the efficient market hypothesis and its political derivative, market fundamentalism. The fallacy in these two intellectual constructs was exposed in a spectacular fashion by the collapse of the financial system. My discovery of a flaw in open society was less spectacular because the concept is less widely accepted, but on a personal level it was equally earthshaking. It forced me to rethink the concept of open society.

I HAVE NOT ABANDONED my belief in the merits of open society, but I realize that it needs stronger arguments to buttress it. Popper took it for granted that in an open society the cognitive function takes precedence over the manipulative function; I now believe that this has to be introduced as an explicit requirement for an open society to flourish. Let me explain how I reached that conclusion.

In a democracy political discourse is aimed not at discovering reality (the cognitive function) but getting elected and staying in power (the manipulative function). Consequently, free political discourse does not necessarily produce more far-sighted policies than an authoritarian regime that suppresses dissent.

To make matters worse, in the political battle to manipulate reality, a commitment to abide by the truth has become a handicap. The Bush administration had at its disposal a powerful right-wing propaganda machine working for it that did not feel any need to respect the facts. This gave it a decided competitive advantage over more old-fashioned political practitioners who were still under the influence of the Enlightenment fallacy and felt constrained by the facts.

Frank Luntz, one of the most successful right-wing propagandists in the United States, openly admitted that he used George Orwell's *1984* as his textbook in devising his slogans. As a believer in the open society, I found this shocking. How could Orwellian Newspeak be as successful in an open society as in a totalitarian state with its Ministry of Truth, which could use Stalinist methods to keep people in line?

This line of enquiry provided me with a clue to the question: what is wrong with America? People are not particularly concerned with the pursuit of truth. They have been conditioned by ever more sophisticated techniques of manipulation to the point where they do not mind being deceived; indeed, they seem to positively invite it.

People have become used to receiving information in prepackaged messages; hence the influence of paid political advertising. They are more interested in being entertained than informed; hence the influence of populist commentators like Bill O'Reilly and Rush Limbaugh.

THE TECHNIQUES OF manipulation have developed gradually over time. They originated in the commercial arena toward the end of the nineteenth century when entrepreneurs discovered that they could improve their profit margins by differentiating their products through branding and advertising. This prompted research into the motivation of consumers, the testing of messages, and the use of focus groups, setting in motion a reflexive process that changed the behavior of the public. It led to the development of a consumer society and spread from there to politics and culture.

These trends undermined the hidden assumptions on which economics and politics were based. Economic theory has taken the conditions of demand and supply as given, and it has shown how free markets under the conditions of perfect competition would lead to the optimum allocation of resources. But the shape of the demand curve was *not* independently given; it was subject to manipulation by advertising. The theory of representative democracy assumed that candidates would present themselves and their programs, and that the electorate would choose the ones they preferred; it did not anticipate that the candidates would study public opinion and then tell the electorate what it wanted to hear. Both of these theories failed to take into account that reality can be manipulated.

The manipulation of reality also became a major theme in the arts. It was literary criticism that eventually led to the development of the postmodern worldview, which turned the Enlightenment upside down. It denied the existence of an objective reality that could be discovered by reason; instead it saw reality as a collection of often contradictory narratives.

I HAD DISMISSED THE postmodern worldview out of hand because it was in conflict with my profound respect for an objective reality. I did not realize the connection between the postmodern worldview and the Bush administration's propaganda machine until an article by Ron Suskind in *New York Times Magazine* opened my eyes. He quoted one of the operators of that machine as saying "when we act, we create our own reality. And while you're studying that reality—judiciously, as you will—we'll act again, creating other new realities."

This forced me to change my mind. I had to take the postmodern position more seriously and recognize it as a fertile fallacy, fully equal in its influence to the Enlightenment, and currently, perhaps, even more influential. But I still regard the postmodern fallacy as more of a fallacy and less fertile than the Enlightenment fallacy. By giving precedence to the manipulative function it ignores the hard core of objective reality that cannot be manipulated. This is more of a defect, in my eyes, than the Enlightenment's neglect of the manipulative function.

ACCORDING TO THE Enlightenment, reason and reality are separate and independent of each other. The only way people can turn reality to their advantage is by understanding the laws that determine the course of events. Under these conditions it could be taken for granted that discovering those laws has to come first. This led to the development of natural science, which is the greatest achievement of the human intellect. It is only in the study of human affairs that the fallacy crept in.

By contrast, the postmodern worldview is *thoroughly* misleading. It has spawned an amoral, pragmatic approach to politics. It can be summed up as follows: Now that we have discovered that reality can be manipulated, why should the cognitive function be given precedence? Why not engage directly in manipulation? Why not pursue power rather than truth?

There is an answer to that argument. While reality can be manipulated, the outcome is bound to diverge from the manipulator's intentions. The divergence needs to be kept to a minimum, and that can be done only through a better understanding of reality. It is this line of reasoning that led me to introduce a commitment to the pursuit of truth as an explicit requirement for open society.

THIS ABSTRACT ARGUMENT can be reinforced by a concrete example. Look at the Bush presidency. It was remarkably successful in manipulating reality. By declaring war on terror it managed to line up the nation behind the president and pave the way to the invasion of Iraq. The invasion was meant to establish the supremacy of the United States in the world, but it achieved the exact opposite result. America lost power and influence precipitously, and George W. Bush is widely considered the worst president the United States has ever had.

This example ought to be convincing. Yet now that the concept of reflexivity is gaining recognition, the danger is that it will be misinterpreted in favor of the postmodern fallacy. A reflexive reality is just too difficult to understand, and people are easily misled by simple answers. It takes a lifetime to understand the argument that a valid prediction does not necessarily prove that the *theory* on which it was based is also true, but a paid political announcement takes only thirty seconds.

It is tempting to adopt the postmodern view of the world, but it is very dangerous to disregard the existence of an objective reality. One way to bring home objective reality is to draw attention to death as a fact of life. The mind finds it difficult to accept the idea of ceasing to exist and all kinds of narratives and myths have sprung up around the idea of life after death. I have been struck by an Aztec ritual in which teams compete in a ball game and the winners are sacrificed to the gods. That is an extreme example of the power of such myths. Yet the fact is that the winning team died.

EVEN SO, I HAVE TO admit that the absence of life after death cannot be proven to those who believe in it. My insistence on the importance of the objective aspect of reality is a matter of personal belief. Indeed, it has a curious resemblance to a religious belief. The objective aspect of reality as I have construed it has many of the attributes of God as conceived in monotheistic religions: it is omnipresent and all-powerful, yet the ways of its working remain somewhat mysterious.

I hold the objective aspect of reality in very high regard, and I used to think that that was the norm. I have come to realize that my attitude is quite unusual and it has to do with my personal history.

The formative experience of my life was the German occupation of Hungary in 1944. Under the wise guidance of my father we not only survived but managed to help others in a situation full of dangers. This turned 1944 into a positive experience for me and gave me an appetite for confronting harsh reality.

This attitude was reinforced by my involvement in the financial markets. I was a risk taker, and I often pushed matters to their limits, though I avoided going over the brink. I learned to protect myself against unpleasant surprises by looking out for all the things that could go wrong. I chose investments that had risk-reward ratios that remained attractive even under the worst assumptions. This made me emphasize the dark side of every situation.

Then I became active with my foundations. Here, the fact that I could do something positive to alleviate injustice increased my willingness to recognize and confront harsh realities. A negative assessment became an invitation for positive involvement.

My foundation ended up devoting much of its resources to seemingly insoluble problems like drug policy and seemingly hopeless cases like Burma, Haiti, Liberia, Sierra Leone, and the Congo. Needless to say, fighting losing battles is not the preferred choice of most foundations.

My commitment to the objective aspect of reality plays the same role in my thinking as religion does in other people's. In the absence of perfect knowledge we need beliefs. I happen to believe in harsh reality, while other people believe in God.

Nevertheless I would argue that when society ignores the objective aspect of reality it does so at its own peril. If we try to avoid unpleasant realities by deceiving ourselves or the electorate, reality will punish us by failing to meet our expectations.

Yes, reality can be manipulated, but the results of our actions are governed not by our desires but by an external reality whose workings we cannot fully comprehend. The better we understand it, the closer the outcome will correspond to our intentions. Understanding reality is the cognitive function. That is why the cognitive function ought to take precedence over and guide the manipulative function. Ignoring an objective reality that cannot be fully understood leads to the postmodern fallacy.

THE FOREGOING DISCOURSE has shown that mankind has adopted two fallacies about the relationship between thinking and reality in recent history: the Enlightenment fallacy and the postmodern fallacy. They are related to each other. The Enlightenment failed to recognize the prevalence of manipulation in the human sphere, and the discovery of the manipulative function led to the postmodern fallacy. Each of them recognizes one half of a complicated relationship.

My conceptual framework, based on the twin principles of fallibility and reflexivity, combines the two halves. Both fallacies have been influential, but my framework has received little acceptance. This goes to show how easy it is to misinterpret reality—much easier than to gain a proper understanding.

The postmodern fallacy is now in the ascendant. It guided the policies of the Bush administration and I note with alarm that it has surfaced in the Obama administration as well. I refer to a recent book by George Akerlof and Robert Shiller, which has been influential in shaping the policies of the Obama administration. That book extols the merits of what the authors call the "confidence multiplier." In other words the authors believe that the ills of the economy can be cured by talking up the financial markets. That belief is half true: the stock market rally has allowed banks to raise capital and it has strengthened the economy in other ways as well. But the confidence multiplier disregards the other half of reflexivity: if reality fails to conform to expectations, confidence can turn into disappointment, boom can turn to bust. I am deeply worried that by deploying the confidence multiplier President Obama has taken ownership of the recession and that if there is a relapse he will be blamed for it.

This discussion should help to clarify my theory of reflexivity by putting it into the context of two false interpretations of reality. In particular, a point that may not have come through loud and clear needs to be emphasized: there is a hard core of objective reality that cannot be manipulated, such as the inevitability of death. It is this hard core that is ignored by the postmodern fallacy.

Emboldened by my recent successes, I will go so far as to claim that my conceptual framework provides the *correct* interpretation of reality. That is a bold claim, and at first sight it seems to be self-contradictory. How can a correct interpretation of reality be reconciled with the principle of inherently imperfect understanding? Easy. By pointing out that reflexivity introduces an element of uncertainty both into the participants' thinking and into the course of events. A framework that claims that the future is inherently uncertain cannot be accused of perfection. Yet it can provide important insights into reality; it can even anticipate the future within bounds, although the bounds themselves are uncertain and variable, as we have seen in the recent financial crisis. By recognizing uncertainty, my framework manages to be both self-consistent and consistent with reality. Yet, since it is less than perfect, it holds itself open to improvement.

Actually, I see a tremendous scope for further development. My original framework, formulated under the influence of Karl Popper, dealt only with the problems of understanding reality. But when I added the requirement that the electorate should cherish truthfulness and punish deception, I entered the realm of values. In that realm, uncertainty is even more prevalent than in the realm of cognition; therefore, a lot more thinking needs to be done.

As we have seen, the truth is difficult to establish and often hard to bear. The path of least resistance leads in the opposite direction, avoiding unpleasant realities and rewarding deception as long as it remains convincing. These tendencies need to be resisted for an open society to remain open and to flourish.

This prescription is particularly relevant to the United States at the present time because that country is facing a particularly unpleasant set of realities in the aftermath of the financial crisis. It has been living beyond its means for the last quarter of a century and making ends meet by borrowing abroad. Now the housing bubble has burst, and consumers are overextended and need to rebuild their savings. The banking system has collapsed and needs to earn its way out of a hole.

The Bush administration had deliberately misled the electorate when it invaded Iraq on false pretenses. The Obama administration cannot be accused of deliberate deception; nevertheless, it has accepted that the country is unwilling to face harsh realities and deployed the confidence multiplier.

Unfortunately, objective reality is unlikely to fulfill the hopes raised by the confidence multiplier. At the same time, the political opposition is not constrained by facts in attacking the president. In these circumstances, the requirement that the electorate should be more committed to the pursuit of truth will be difficult to meet. It provides a good agenda for my foundation, but the current state of democracy in America does not strengthen the case for open society as a superior form of social organization. I need to find a stronger argument.

A better case can be found by reverting to the Founding Fathers, who formed their views long before the concept of open society was introduced. The Founding Fathers built their case on the value of individual freedom. The epistemological argument they employed was flawed: the Declaration of Independence states that "We hold these truths to be self-evident," but there is nothing self-evident about them. Self-evident or not, however, the value of individual freedom is enduring and, having been exposed to totalitarian regimes, I'm passionately devoted to it. And I am not alone.

Reverting to the Founding Fathers has another great advantage: it allows a discussion of power relations. The Constitution protected against tyranny by a division of powers. The division of powers recognizes that there are competing interests and different interpretations of reality within society that need to be reconciled by a political process. The constitutional checks and balances preclude the formation of absolute power that could claim to be in possession of the ultimate truth. The Constitution establishes a mechanism whereby different branches of government interact and control each other. But that is not sufficient.

Open society can prevail only when people can speak truth to power. It needs the rule of law that guarantees freedom of speech and press, freedom of association and assembly, and other rights and freedoms. They empower citizens to defend themselves against the abuse of power and to make use of the judicial branch for such defense. That is how the Founding Fathers created an open society.

Let me spell out my conclusion more clearly. Open society is a desirable form of social organization both as a means to an end and as an end in itself. It enables a society to understand the problems confronting it and to deal with them more successfully then other forms of social organizations, *provided* it gives precedence to the cognitive function over the manipulative function and the people are willing to confront harsh realities.

In other words, the *instrumental* value of democracy is conditional on the electorate's commitment to the pursuit of truth, and in that regard the current performance of American democracy does not live up to its past achievements. We cannot rely on the inherent superiority of the American system and need to prove ourselves anew. But quite apart from its instrumental value, open society also has an intrinsic value, namely, the freedom of the individual, which applies whether open society flourishes or not. For instance, it applied in the Soviet Union.

Of course, the freedom of the individual must be made compatible with the public interest and the freedom of other individuals.

Moreover, the intrinsic value of individual freedom falls short of being self-evident. For instance, it is not generally recognized in China, where the interests of the collective take precedence over the interests of the individual. This was the clear message of the opening ceremony of the 2008 Olympic Games. The ceremony showed that by doing exactly what they are told at exactly the right time, a large collection of individuals can produce a superb spectacle.

With the changing power relations between the United States and China, the value of individual freedom is likely to assume increasing importance in the immediate future. I will address that subject in my last lecture.

Thank you.

LECTURE FOUR

Capitalism Versus Open Society

Central European University Lecture Series,

October 26–30, 2009

TODAY I WANT TO explore the conflict between capitalism and open society, market values and social values. I am going to approach the subject indirectly by first introducing a phenomenon that has attracted my attention only recently, but has assumed such importance in my thinking that I could almost call it the fourth pillar of my conceptual framework. That phenomenon is the agency problem: Agents are supposed to represent the interests of their principals, but in fact, they tend to put their own interests ahead of the interests of those whom they are supposed to represent.

The agency problem has been extensively analyzed by economists, but they look at it exclusively in terms of contracts and incentives and they largely disregard questions of ethics and values. Yet if you leave out ethical considerations the problem becomes pretty well intractable; values like honesty and integrity lose their grip on people's behavior and people become increasingly motivated by economic incentives.

By claiming to be value-free, market fundamentalism has actually undermined moral values.

Markets are supposed to be guided by an invisible hand; that is what makes them so efficient. Participants need to exercise no moral judgments in reaching their buy and sell decisions because their actions are not supposed to have any visible influence on market prices.

In truth, the rules governing financial markets are decided by the visible hand of politicians, and in a representative democracy politicians run into an agency problem.

Thus, the agency problem poses grave difficulties for both representative democracy and the market economy that cannot be resolved without an appeal to moral principles. That is how the agency problem has gained such prominence in my thinking. First, I will analyze the agency problem and then I will deal with the conflict between capitalism and open society.

LET ME START AT the beginning. I first encountered the agency problem in connection with the so-called resource curse. "Resource curse" refers to the tendency of countries that are rich in natural resources to be cursed with corrupt or repressive governments, insurrections, and civil wars so that the people are even poorer and lead more miserable lives than in countries that are less well endowed by nature. Think of the Congo, Sudan, Sierra Leone, and Liberia.

One of the nongovernmental organizations I support, Global Witness, proposed a campaign based on the slogan "Publish What You Pay." The idea was to get oil companies and mining companies to disclose the payments they make to various governments. The amounts could then be added up and the governments could be held accountable by the people for the monies they received.

The campaign was launched in 2002 and it has had an interesting history. The idea itself turned out to be a fertile fallacy because, although public opinion could put enough pressure on the big oil companies, fly-by-night operators and companies domiciled in nondemocratic states were less susceptible. So the amounts could not be added up.

Fortunately, the British government took up the cause and formed the Extractive Industries Transparency Initiative, which brought together governments, companies, and civil society in an effort to establish international standards of transparency that apply to companies and to governments alike. In those countries that subscribed to the transparency initiative, the governments undertook the task of publishing the amounts they received. Countries like Nigeria and Azerbaijan are seeing positive results.

In analyzing the resource curse, I came to attribute great importance to what I called an "asymmetric agency problem." According to the modern concept of sovereignty, the natural resources of a country belong to the people of that country, but governments, which are supposed to be agents of the people, put their own interests ahead of the interests of the people whom they are supposed to represent, and they engage in all sorts of corrupt practices. On the opposite side, the managements of international oil and mining companies represent the interests of the companies all too well. They used to go so far as to bribe governments in order to obtain concessions. Willing takers and givers of bribes are the root cause of the resource curse.

Once I became aware of the agency problem, I discovered it everywhere. Communism failed because of the agency problem. Karl Marx's proposition about everybody contributing according to their ability and receiving according to their need was a very attractive idea, but the Communist rulers put their own interests ahead of the interests of the people.

The agency problem is also the bane of representative democracy; the elected representatives use their powers for their own interests to the detriment of the common interest.

And in the recent financial crisis, the agency problem proved to be the undoing of the financial system. When financial engineers turned mortgages into securities by issuing collateralized debt obligations, or CDOs, they thought they were reducing risk through geographical diversification. In reality, they were introducing a new risk by separating the interests of the agents who created and distributed the synthetic instruments from the interest of the owners of those securities. The agents were more interested in earning fees than in protecting the interests of the principals.

So the agency problem seemed ubiquitous.

Yet, in spite of its pervasive influence, it escaped attention until relatively recently. In my student days it was almost totally unrecognized. In the last twenty years it has received more attention, but, again, mainly from economists who studied it in terms of contracts and incentives. In reality, the agency problem is more of an ethical problem, and analyzing it in terms of contracts and incentives actually aggravated the ethical problem. Establishing the principle that people's behavior is governed by contracts and incentives had the effect of eliminating, or at least diminishing, ethical considerations. That may sound perverse, but only because reflexivity is not well understood.

VALUES ARE LESS CLOSELY governed by an objective reality than cognitive notions; therefore, they are more easily shaped by the theories that people adopt and economic theory is a case in point.

Markets are supposed to act as an invisible hand, bringing demand and supply into balance. What makes the invisible hand so efficient is that there is no need to exercise moral judgment; all values can be expressed in terms of money, and money is fungible. "*Pecunia non olet*—money doesn't smell," the Romans used to say. But taking it for granted that all human behavior is guided by self-interest leaves no room for the exercise of moral judgment—and society cannot exist without some ethical precepts.

The behavior of market participants is guided by market values, and market values are quite different in character from the moral values that are supposed to guide the behavior of people as members of society. This opens up a whole range of questions that I have not been able to resolve concerning the conflict between market values and social values. The agency problem has provided me with some new insights. I was also inspired by a short monograph by Bruce R. Scott, *The Concept of Capitalism* (Springer, 2009). As a result, I may have something new to say. Indeed, I myself am shocked by some of the conclusions I have reached.

Scott argues that capitalism has been misinterpreted by conflating it with the market mechanism. This is a distortion that Scott attributes mainly to Milton Friedman; I am less specific and attribute it to market fundamentalism. Scott argues further that behind the invisible hand of the market lurks the visible hand of human agency, namely the political process, which sets and administers the rules. That is where the agency problem comes into play, and so does the conflict between market values and social values.

The United States is a democratic, open society based on the freedom of the individual, who is protected by the rule of law as defined by the Constitution. At the same time, the American economy is based on the market mechanism, which allows individuals to engage in free exchange without undue interference from arbitrary actions by governmental authority. The political and economic arrangements seem to fit together seamlessly. One could easily speak of an open society and a market economy in the same breath, and people, including me, often do. But appearances are deceptive. There is a deep-seated conflict between capitalism and open society, market values and social values. The conflict has been successfully covered up by the market fundamentalist ideology, which gained the upper hand in the 1980s during Ronald Reagan's presidency.

The distinguishing feature of the market mechanism is that it is *amoral*: one person's dollar is worth exactly the same as another person's, irrespective of how she came to possess it. That is what makes markets so efficient: participants need not worry about moral considerations. In an efficient market, individual decisions affect market prices only marginally: if one person abstained from participating as either buyer or seller, someone else would take her place with only a marginal difference in the price. Therefore individual market participants bear little responsibility for the outcome. Amoral is easily confused with immoral. I am often asked, particularly by student audiences, whether I feel guilty about having made so much money on the stock market. When I explain that, prior to becoming a public figure who can, in fact, influence markets, moral considerations did not enter my decision-making process, I am often met with incomprehension.

But markets are suitable only for individual choices, not for social decisions. They allow individual participants to engage in free exchange; but they are not designed to exercise social choices such as deciding the rules that should govern society, including how the market mechanism should function. That is the purview of politics. Extending the idea of a free-standing market, self-governing and self-correcting, to the political sphere is highly deceptive because it removes ethical considerations from politics, which cannot properly function without them.

In the United States politics takes the form of representative democracy. People elect representatives who operate the levers of power. People elected to office are agents who are supposed to represent the interests of the people. In reality, they tend to put their own interests ahead of the interests of the people. Getting elected is expensive, and representatives are beholden to their supporters. Those who don't play the game don't get elected. That is how money pollutes politics and special interests trump the public interest.

The agency problem in the American political system is not

new. It is inherent in a representative democracy. The right to petition elected representatives was written into the Constitution. Yet the agency problem seems to be much more severe today than it was even as recently as my arrival in the United States in 1956. Why?

There are some objective historical developments that may be held partly responsible, notably the growth of special interests and the development of sophisticated methods of manipulating public opinion, but the main culprit is a decline in public morality fostered by the rise of market fundamentalism.

I would like to think that at the time of the founding of the republic, citizens were genuinely guided by a sense of civic virtue. Fortunately, the Founding Fathers did not put much faith in that and built the Constitution on the division of powers: they created checks and balances between competing interests. That is why the Constitution holds up so well in spite of the decline in morality. Even when I first arrived, in 1956, people professed to be guided by intrinsic values like honesty and integrity. It may have been hypocritical with all kinds of vices clandestinely practiced, but still, it was very different from today's public life, in which the blatant pursuit of self-interest is openly admitted and people are admired for success, irrespective of how they achieved it.

I do not want to be misunderstood. Painting too rosy a picture of the past is characteristic of people of a certain age, and I do not want to fall into such an obvious trap. I do not claim that politicians were more honest or society was more just in 1956. America has made great progress since then in transparency, accountability, and social equality. But there has been a remarkable transformation in what behavior is socially acceptable and even admirable due to the rise of market fundamentalism. I describe it as a decline in public morality in the very special sense that the *amorality* of market values has penetrated into areas where it does not properly belong.

I DEFINE MARKET fundamentalism as the undue extension of market values to other spheres of social life, notably politics. Economic theory claims that in conditions of general equilibrium, the invisible hand assures the optimum allocation of resources. This means that people pursuing their self-interest are indirectly also serving the public interest. It gives self-interest and the profit motive a moral imprimatur that allows them to replace virtues like honesty, integrity, and concern for others.

The argument is invalid on several counts. First, financial markets do not tend toward equilibrium. General equilibrium theory reached its conclusions by taking the conditions of supply and demand as independently given. The invisible hand of the market then brings supply and demand into equilibrium. This approach ignores the reflexive feedback loops between market prices and the underlying conditions of supply and demand. It also ignores the visible hand of the political process, which lies hidden behind the market mechanism.

Second, general equilibrium theory takes the initial allocation of resources as given. This rules out any consideration of social justice. Most importantly, the theory assumes that people know what their self-interest is and how best to pursue it. In reality, there is a significant gap between what people think and what the facts are.

NEVERTHELESS, market fundamentalism has emerged triumphant. How could that happen?

One reason is that the main policy implication of market fundamentalism—that government interference in the economy should be kept to a minimum—is not as unsound as the arguments employed to justify it. The market mechanism may be flawed, but the political process is even more so. Participants in the political process are even more fallible than market participants because politics revolves around social values, whereas markets take the participants' values as given. As we have seen, social values are highly susceptible to manipulation. Moreover, politics are poisoned by the agency problem. To guard against the agency problem, all kinds of safeguards have to be introduced, and this makes the behavior of governmental authorities in the economic sphere much more rigid and bureaucratic than the behavior of private participants. On all these grounds, it makes sense to argue that governmental interference in the economy should be kept to a minimum.

So market fundamentalism has merely substituted an invalid argument for what could have been a much stronger one. It could have argued that all human constructs are imperfect and social choices involve choosing the lesser evil, and on those grounds government intervention in the economy should be kept to a minimum. That would have been a reasonable position. Instead, it claimed that the failures of government intervention proved that free markets are perfect. That is simply bad logic.

I want to make myself quite clear: I condemn market fundamentalism as a false and dangerous doctrine, but I am in favor of keeping government intervention and regulations to a minimum for other, better, reasons.

By far the most powerful force working in favor of market fundamentalism is that it serves the self-interests of the owners and managers of capital. The distribution of wealth is taken as given, and the pursuit of self-interest is found to serve the common interest. What more could those who are in control of capital ask for? They constitute a wealthy and powerful group, well positioned to promote market fundamentalism not only by cognitive arguments but also by the active manipulation of public opinion. Market fundamentalism endows the market mechanism, which is amoral by nature, with a moral character and turns the pursuit of self-interest into a civic virtue similar to the pursuit of truth. It has prevailed by the force of manipulation, not by the force of reason. It is supported by a powerful and well-financed propaganda machine that distorts the public's understanding of its own self-interests. For example, how else could the campaign to repeal the estate tax, which applies only to an elite 1 percent of the population, have been so successful?

There are, of course, competing forces in that arena using similar methods of manipulation, but they tend to be less well financed because they cannot draw on the self-interest of the wealthiest and most powerful segment of the population. That is how market fundamentalism emerged triumphant in the last twenty-five years and why even the financial crisis was not sufficient to impair its influence. This was demonstrated by President Obama's decision to avoid recapitalizing the banks in a way that would have given the government majority control.

Market fundamentalism should not be conflated with the efficient market hypothesis. You can be an economist working with that hypothesis without being a market fundamentalist. Indeed, many economists are bleeding-heart liberals. But the efficient market hypothesis has a stranglehold on the teaching of economics in American universities, and that phenomenon can be attributed to the financial support given by capitalists and foundations committed to market fundamentalism. Those groups are also responsible for the encroachment of market values into other disciplines, such as law and political science.

Capitalism is not directly opposed to open society the way Soviet communism was. Nevertheless, it poses some serious threats. I have already discussed one of them: financial markets are not equilibrium-bound but bubble-prone. The dismantling of the regulatory mechanism has given rise to a super-bubble whose bursting will negatively influence the American economy for several years to come. This discussion has revealed another threat to open society: the agency problem and the influence of money in politics, which contaminate the political process.

In an open society the political process is supposed to serve the common interest; in contemporary America, the political process has been captured by special interests. Our elected representatives are beholden to those who finance their election, not to the electorate at large. What is happening to President Obama's healthcare and energy bills provides a vivid illustration. The electorate has been brainwashed to such an extent that a responsible discussion of the public good has become well-nigh impossible. A national health service and a carbon tax are nonstarters. Our choices are confined to solutions that can be gamed by special interests.

Lobbying is at the core of the agency problem. How can it be brought under control?

This is an ethical issue and not a matter of modifying economic incentives. Lobbying is lucrative, and it is liable to remain so even if the rules are tightened. In the absence of moral values, regulations can always be circumvented; what is worse, the regulations themselves will be designed to serve special interests, not the common interest. That is the danger facing the United States today, when a wounded financial sector is seeking to regain its former preeminence.

THERE IS A WAY TO deal with the ethical issue. We need to draw a clear distinction between the economic and political spheres. Market participation and rule making are two different functions. Markets allow participants to engage in free exchange. Here it is quite legitimate for participants to be guided by the profit motive. By contrast, the making and enforcement of rules ought to be guided by consideration of the public good. Here the profit motive is misplaced. It is when people try to bend the rules to their own advantage that the political process becomes corrupted and representative democracy fails to produce the results that would make open society a desirable form of social organization. It should be emphasized that this argument directly contradicts the currently fashionable market fundamentalist attitude, which speaks of a political marketplace.

How could the political process be improved in an open society? I propose a rather simple rule: people should separate their role as market participants from their role as political participants. As market participants we ought to pursue our self-interest; as participants in the political process we ought to be guided by the public interest. The justification for this rule is also rather simple. In conditions of close-to-perfect competition, no single competitor can affect the outcome; therefore individual market decisions have no effect on social conditions, whether or not one cares about the common good. But political decisions do affect social conditions; therefore it makes all the difference whether or not they serve the public interest.

The trouble is that the public good cannot be determined by reference to a generally accepted objective standard. It is contingent on the views of the electorate, but in the absence of an objective standard, those views are easily manipulated. And manipulation is self-reinforcing; the more outrageous the political claims and counter claims, the harder it is to tell what is right and what is wrong. That is what has made the political process so ineffective.

By contrast, the market mechanism functions much better. People may not know what is good for them, but profits do provide an objective criterion by which market participants' performance can be measured. No wonder that the profit motive has gained such prominence among the values that guide people's behavior. Not only does profit provide the means for the pursuit of whatever ends people may have, but it also serves as an end in itself because as a reliable measure of success they attract other people's admiration and generate self-esteem. Indeed, many successful business people feel much more secure in making money than in using their wealth.

THE SPREAD OF MARKET values has brought immense economic benefits. Looking back in history, Christianity used to treat the pursuit of profit as sinful. This hampered economic development. The Reformation then facilitated the development of markets and opened the way to material progress and the accumulation of wealth. Society underwent a great transformation. Traditional relationships were replaced by contractual ones. Contractual relationships came to penetrate into more and more spheres of social life, and eventually relationships started to be replaced by transactions. The pace of change began to accelerate; it has sped up tremendously just during my lifetime.

The difference between my childhood in Hungary and my adult life in America is quite dramatic, and the changes that have occurred in America between my arrival in 1956 and the present day are dramatic as well. When I first came to America I was struck by how much further market values had penetrated into society than in my native Hungary, or even England, where traditional values and class distinctions still prevailed. Since then, both England and America have undergone a further transformation. The professions—such as medicine, law, and journalism—became businesses. In my view, this has had a destabilizing effect on society just as market fundamentalism has had a destabilizing effect on financial markets.

Exactly what level of stability is socially desirable is, of course, a matter of opinion. The proper role of the profit motive in the professions is similarly open to debate. But there can be *no question* that the profit motive has had a nefarious influence in the political sphere because it has aggravated the agency problem.

HOW CAN THE AGENCY problem be minimized? It is too much to expect those who have a vital special interest at stake not to lobby Congress; the tobacco industry is bound to oppose legislation against cigarettes, and the insurance industry will be against a single-payer healthcare system. But those who do not have a vital interest at stake ought to give precedence to the public interests over their narrow self-interests. They need not be bothered by the so-called free-rider problem, namely that others who act more selfishly would also benefit from their unselfish behavior—because the objective of the exercise *is* to benefit the public.

To sum up, in my previous lecture I argued that the cognitive function ought to be given precedence over the manipulative function. In this lecture, I argued that while the profit motive is perfectly justified within the existing rules, when it comes to making the rules, the public interest ought to be given precedence over personal interests. I firmly believe that even if a small portion of the electorate met these two requirements, representative democracy would function better.

I SHOULD LIKE TO END on a personal note. I have practiced what I preach. As a hedge fund manager I have played by the rules and tried to maximize my profits. As a citizen I try to improve the rules, even if the reforms go against my personal interests. For example, I support the regulation of hedge funds along with other financial institutions. I firmly believe that if more people followed this precept, our political system would function much better. I also believe that foundations like mine can play an important role exactly because so few people follow that precept.

At my foundation, the Open Society Institute, we have made it our business to protect the public interest against the encroachments of private interests. We are also supporting their civil society efforts to hold governments accountable. I would describe these endeavors as political philanthropy. It can, I believe, make a greater contribution toward making the world a better place than conventional philanthropy because fewer people are engaged in it.

I am in a privileged position. I am more independent than most people because I don't depend on clients or customers, and I feel that I am under a moral obligation to put my privileged position to good use. I am, of course, heavily outgunned by special interests, but at least I have the satisfaction that my money has greater scarcity value.

The trouble is that special interests also seek to disguise themselves as protectors of the public interest, and it takes a discerning eye to discriminate between the genuine and the phony, especially since both sides are forced to resort to similar methods of persuasion. In the absence of objective criteria, one can reach a judgment only by a process of trial and error. People of good intentions engaged on one side of the debate often find it difficult to believe that there are people on the other side with equally good intentions. The best way to find out is by taking their claims at face value and engaging them on the substance of their argument. This has the beneficial effect of giving the cognitive function precedence in the political debate. Only if they fail to respond in kind should they be dismissed and subsequently ignored. There are people like that in every country; unfortunately in the United States they are *not* ignored. They have become very influential. Whether the electorate refuses to be influenced by people who try to manipulate them with total disregard for the truth is the test that every open society has to pass to remain open. Given the success of Orwellian propaganda, America is not doing well in this regard.

The political process that has served America well for two centuries seems to have deteriorated. We used to have two parties competing for the middle, but the middle ground has shrunk and politics have become increasingly polarized. President Obama has done his level best to reverse the trend—he has tried to be a great unifier, but to no avail.

In the end, how a democracy functions depends on the people who live in it. I believe that if more people separated their role as political participants from their role as market participants, American democracy would function better. It is up to each individual. That is what I have done. Even a small minority could be helpful in rebuilding the vanishing middle ground.

Thank you.

LECTURE FIVE

THE WAY AHEAD

Central European University Lecture Series,

October 26–30, 2009

IN THESE LECTURES I have offered a conceptual framework for a better understanding of human events. These events are not determined by timelessly valid scientific laws. Such laws exist, of course, but they are not sufficient to determine the course of events. The complexity of the situations is one reason, and the role of the participants' thinking is another.

I have focused on the reflexive, two-way connection between the participants' thinking and reality, and I have emphasized the causal role that misunderstandings and misconceptions play in shaping reality. Both of these influences have been strangely ignored. They introduce an element of uncertainty into the subject matter that, except in the simplest situations, makes it impossible to predict the future.

One can still sketch out various plausible scenarios and evaluate their likelihood. One can also prescribe desirable outcomes. I have done both, many times. Indeed, I can claim to have specialized in it, focusing on predictions as an investor and prescriptions as a philanthropist. I have been successful enough in the former to be able to afford the latter. I should like to devote today's discussion to this dual task.

WE ARE AT A MOMENT in history when the range of uncertainties is unusually wide. We have just passed through the worst financial crisis since World War II. It is quantitatively much larger and qualitatively different from other financial crises. The only relevant comparisons are with the Japanese real estate bubble, which burst in 1991 and from which Japan has still not recovered, and with the Great Depression of the 1930s. What differentiates this crisis from the Japanese experience is that the latter was confined to a single country; this crisis has involved the entire world. What differentiates it from the Great Depression is that this time the financial system was not allowed to collapse but was put on artificial life support.

In fact, the magnitude of the credit and leverage problem we face today is even greater than in the 1930s. In 1929, total credit outstanding in the United States was 160 percent of GDP and it rose to 250 percent by 1932; in 2008 we started at 365 percent—and this calculation does not take into account the pervasive use of derivatives, which was absent in the 1930s. And yet, in spite of that, the artificial life support has been successful. Barely a year after the bankruptcy of Lehman Brothers, financial markets have stabilized, stock markets have rebounded, and the economy is showing signs of recovery. People want to return to business as usual and think of the crash of 2008 as a bad dream.

I regret to tell you that the recovery is liable to run out of steam and may even be followed by a "double dip," although I am not sure whether it will occur in 2010 or 2011.

My views are far from unique, but they are at variance with the prevailing mood. The longer the turnaround lasts, the more people will come to believe in it, but in my judgment, the prevailing mood is far removed from reality. This is characteristic of far-from-equilibrium situations, in which perceptions tend to lag behind reality. To complicate matters, the lag works in both directions. Most people have not yet realized that this crisis is different from previous ones—that we are at the end of an era. Others—including me—failed to anticipate the extent of the rebound.

The confusion is not confined to the financial sphere; it extends to the entire international arena.

After the collapse of the Soviet empire the United States

emerged as the sole superpower. No other power, or combination of powers, could challenge its supremacy. But the uni-polar world order did not take root. When President Bush sought to assert America's supremacy by invading Iraq on false pretences, he achieved the exact opposite of what he intended. The United States suffered a precipitous decline in its power and influence. So the disarray in the international financial system is matched by instability in international relations. The new world order that will eventually emerge will not be dominated by the United States to the same extent as the old one.

To understand what is happening we need a different conceptual framework from the one to which we have been accustomed. The efficient market hypothesis looks at financial markets in isolation and totally disregards politics. But that gives a distorted picture. As I have pointed out several times, behind the invisible hand of markets there is the *visible* hand of politics, which establishes the rules and conditions in which the market mechanism operates. My conceptual framework relates to the political economy, not the market economy as an abstract construct that is governed by timelessly valid laws. I look at financial markets as a branch of history.

THE INTERNATIONAL FINANCIAL system, as it was reconstructed after the Second World War, did not create a level playing field; it was lopsided by design. The international financial institutions—

the International Monetary Fund and the World Bank—were organized as shareholding companies in which rich countries held a disproportionate share of the votes and also controlled the boards. This put the countries at the periphery at a disadvantage vis-à-vis those at the center.

Ever since, the system has been dominated by the United States. At the Bretton Woods conference John Maynard Keynes proposed, but it was the head of the American delegation, Harry White, who disposed. Since then we have gone from an almost completely regulated system to an almost completely deregulated one; the changes were led by the United States, and the system has continued to be guided by what has become known as the Washington Consensus.

Although the rules laid down by the Washington Consensus are supposed to apply to all countries equally, the United States—as the issuer of the main international currency—is "more equal" than the others. Effectively, the international financial system has a two-tier structure: countries that can borrow in their own currency constitute the center, and those whose borrowings are denominated in one of the hard currencies constitute the periphery. If individual countries get into difficulties, they receive assistance, but only under strict conditions. That holds true whether they are from the center or from the periphery. But if the center itself becomes endangered, then preserving the system takes precedence over all other considerations.

That happened for the first time in the international banking crisis of 1982. If the debtor countries had been allowed to default, the banking system would have collapsed. Therefore, the international financial authorities banded together and introduced what I called at the time "the collective system of lending." The lenders were induced to roll over their loans and the debtor countries were lent enough additional money to service their debts. The net effect was that debtor countries fell into severe recession—Latin America lost a decade of growth—but the banking system was allowed to earn its way out of a hole. When the banks built up sufficient reserves, the loans were restructured into what became known as Brady bonds and the banks were able to write off their remaining losses.

Something similar happened in 1997, but by then the banks had learned to securitize their loans so they could not be forced into a collective system of lending, and most of the losses had to be taken by the debtor countries. This set the pattern: the debtor countries were subjected to harsh market discipline, but when the system itself was in danger, the normal rules were suspended—banks, whose collective failure would have endangered the system, were bailed out.

The financial crisis of 2007–2008 was different because it originated at the center and the periphery countries were drawn into it only after the bankruptcy of Lehman Brothers. The IMF was faced with a novel task: to protect the periphery from a storm that originated at the center. It did not have enough capital, but member countries banded together and raised a trillion dollars. Even so, the IMF has had some difficulties in coping with the situation; it was designed to deal with problems in the public sector, and the shortage of credit was affecting mainly the private sector. But on the whole, the IMF adapted itself to its novel task remarkably well.

Overall, the international financial authorities have handled this crisis the same way previous crises have been handled: they bailed out the failing institutions and applied monetary and fiscal stimulus. But this crisis was much bigger and the same techniques did not work so well. The rescue of Lehman Brothers failed. That was a game-changing event; financial markets actually ceased to function and had to be put on artificial life support. This meant that governments had to effectively guarantee that no other institution whose failure could endanger the system would be allowed to fail. That is when the crisis spread to the periphery, because periphery countries could not provide equally credible guarantees. This time it was Eastern Europe that was the worst hit. The countries at the center used the balance sheets of their central banks to pump money into the system and to guarantee the liabilities of commercial banks, and governments engaged in deficit financing to stimulate the economy on an unprecedented scale.

These measures have been successful, and the global economy appears to be stabilizing. There is a growing belief that the global financial system has once again escaped collapse and we are slowly returning to business as usual. This is a grave misinterpretation of the current situation. Humpty Dumpty cannot be put together again. Let me explain why.

THE GLOBALIZATION OF financial markets that has taken place since the 1980s was a market fundamentalist project spearheaded by the United States and the United Kingdom. Allowing financial capital to move around freely in the world made it difficult to tax it or to regulate it. This put financial capital into a privileged position. Governments had to pay more attention to the requirements of international capital than to the aspirations of their own people because financial capital could move around more freely. So as a market fundamentalist project, globalization was highly successful; individual countries found it difficult to resist it. But the global financial system that emerged was fundamentally unstable because it was built on the false premise that financial markets can be safely left to their own devices. That is why it broke down, and that is why it cannot be put together again.

Global markets need global regulations, but the regulations that are currently in force are rooted in the principle of national sovereignty. There are some international agreements, most notably the Basel Accords on minimum capital requirements, and there is also good cooperation among market regulators. But the source of the authority is always the sovereign state. This means that it is not enough to restart a mechanism that has stalled; we need to create a regulatory mechanism that has never existed. As things stand now, the financial system of each country is being sustained and supported by its own government. The governments are primarily concerned with their own economies. This tends to give rise to financial protectionism, which threatens to disrupt and perhaps destroy global financial markets. British regulators will never again rely on the Icelandic authorities, and countries at the periphery will be reluctant to be entirely dependent on foreign-owned banks.

The point I am trying to make is that regulations must be international in scope. Without this, financial markets cannot remain global; they would be destroyed by regulatory arbitrage. Businesses would move to the countries where the regulatory climate is the most benign, and this would expose other countries to risks they cannot afford to run. Globalization was so successful because it forced all countries to remove regulations, but the process does not work in reverse. It will be difficult to get countries to agree on uniform regulations. Different countries have different interests that drive them toward different solutions.

THIS CAN BE SEEN in Europe. And if European countries cannot agree among themselves, how can the rest of the world? During the crisis, Europe could not reach a Europewide agreement on guaranteeing its financial system; each country had to guarantee its own. As things stand now, the euro is an incomplete currency. It has a common central bank but it does not have a common treasury—and guaranteeing or injecting equity into banks is a treasury function. The crisis offered an opportunity to remedy this shortfall, but Germany stood in the way.

Germany used to be the driving force behind European integration, but that was at a time when Germany was willing to pay practically any price for reunification. Today's Germany is very different. It is at odds with the rest of the world in fearing inflation rather than recession and, above all, it does not want to serve as the deep pocket for the rest of Europe. Without a driving force, European integration has ground to a halt.

Fortunately, Europe had the benefit of the social safety net. This held down European growth rates in good times, but it served its purpose in the downturn and so the recession in Euroland turned out to be less severe than expected. Now that the fears of an economic collapse have subsided, the European Union is showing some signs of political revival. The European Central Bank has effectively bailed out the Irish banking system and Ireland has resoundingly endorsed the Lisbon Treaty. Unfortunately the political revival of the European Union is likely to be as anemic as the economic one.

THE FACT THAT THE financial crisis is having different long-term effects on different countries may also turn out to be a problem. In the short term, all countries were negatively affected, but in the long term there will be winners and losers. Although the range of uncertainties for the actual course of events is very wide, shifts in relative positions can be predicted with greater certainty. To put it bluntly, the United States stands to lose the most and China is poised to emerge as the greatest winner. The extent of the shift is already exceeding most expectations. There will be significant changes in the relative positions of other countries as well, but from a global perspective the one between the United States and China is the most significant.

The United States has been at the center of the international financial system ever since the Second World War. The dollar has served as the main international currency, and the United States has derived immense benefits from it, but lately it has abused its privilege. Starting in the 1980s it has built up an ever-increasing current account deficit. This could have continued indefinitely because the Asian tigers, first under the leadership of Japan and then of China, were willing to finance that deficit by building up their dollar holdings. But the excessive indebtedness of United States households brought the process to an end. When the housing bubble burst, households found themselves overextended. The banking system has suffered tremendous losses and has to earn its way out of a hole. In commercial real estate and leveraged buyouts, the bloodletting is yet to come. These factors will continue to weigh on the American economy, and the American consumer will no longer be able to serve as the motor for the world economy.

To some extent, China may be able to take its place. China has been the primary beneficiary of globalization, and it has been largely insulated from the financial crisis.

For the West in general, and the United States in particular, the crisis was an internally generated event that led to the collapse of the financial system. For China, it was an external shock that hurt exports but left the financial, political, and economic systems unscathed.

China has discovered a remarkably efficient method of unleashing the creative, acquisitive, and entrepreneurial energies of the people. They are allowed to pursue their self-interest while the state can skim off a significant portion of the surplus value of their labor by maintaining an undervalued currency and accumulating a trade surplus. So China is likely to emerge as the big winner.

China is not a democracy, and its rulers know that they must avoid social unrest if they want to remain the rulers. Therefore, they will do anything in their power to maintain economic growth at 8 percent and to create new jobs for a growing workforce. And they have plenty of power because of the trade surplus. China can stimulate its domestic economy through infrastructure investments, and it can foster its exports by investing in and extending credits to its trading partners. After all, that is what China was doing when it was financing its exports to America by buying U.S. government bonds. Now that American consumers have to cut back, China can develop relations with other countries. So while the United States limps along China will be a positive force in the world economy.

The Chinese economy is, of course, much smaller than that of the United States. With a smaller motor, the world economy is likely to move forward at a slower pace. But within these limits a tectonic shift is taking place between the United States and China, with third parties reorienting themselves toward the source of positive impulses. The shift may not be permanent or irreversible—just think of the rise and fall of Japan Inc.—but at the present moment, it constitutes the most predictable and significant trend in the global political economy, and China is pulling along its trading partners, such as Brazil and some African and Asian countries. India is doing well based on domestic growth.

The success of Chinese economic policy cannot be taken for granted. The infrastructure investment in the Chinese hinterland may not generate self-sustaining economic growth. Under the Chinese system, the return on new investments is generally very low because investment decisions are dictated by political rather than commercial considerations. On the two previous occasions when bank credit was relaxed, the result was a spate of bad loans. This time it may be different because there has been a shift in power from the regional to the central authorities, and the local officials of the banks are no longer under the control of the provincial authorities. But again, success cannot be taken for granted. Moreover, China may be dragged down by a global slowdown. But if China flounders, the global economy will lose its motor. Therefore, the relative success of China is more assured than its absolute success.

We are at a moment in history that, in some ways, is comparable to the end of the Second World War. Then, the prevailing system had actually collapsed and a new one had to be built from scratch. At Bretton Woods, the victorious powers proved equal to the task. Inspired mainly by Lord Keynes, they built a system that could accommodate the entire world even if the United States occupied a privileged position. Today, the prevailing multilateral system—call it "international capitalism"—has not fully collapsed, but it has been greatly weakened, its inherent flaws have been revealed, and it is challenged by a viable alternative. The rise of China offers a form of economic organization that is fundamentally different from the current international financial system. It may be given the label "state capitalism," and it is distinct from the international capitalism championed by the Washington Consensus. We are at the end of an era, but we are not fully aware of it.

The two forms of economic organization—state capitalism and international capitalism—are in competition with each other. Neither of them is attractive. The Washington Consensus has failed. International capitalism in its present form has proven itself inherently unstable because it lacks adequate regulation. It is also highly unjust, favoring the haves over the have nots.

At the same time, an international system based on state capitalism would inevitably lead to conflicts between states. The first signs of conflict are already beginning to surface because, ironically, China is repeating the mistakes of the colonial powers in its dealings with the countries that are rich in natural resources—and this just at the time when the colonial powers have learned from their mistakes and are trying to rectify them. In order to gain access to natural resources, China is dealing with the rulers and neglecting the people. This helps oppressive and corrupt regimes to stay in power. This is an undesirable outcome, but China is not the only one to be blamed for it. When a Chinese company tried to buy Unocal, it was rebuffed. And more recently, Rio Tinto reneged on a deal to sell an interest to a Chinese company. This has pushed China into dealing with those countries that the international financial institutions have shunned; among them, Burma, Sudan, Zimbabwe, the Congo, and Angola stand out. Guinea is the latest example. This is becoming a source of considerable friction, which is not in the best interests of China, let alone the rest of the world. But China considers itself the aggrieved party and remains reluctant to join the Extractive Industries Transparency Initiative. This has become the biggest obstacle to the continued success of that initiative.

While the prevailing multilateral system will try to reconstitute itself, China will expand on a bilateral basis. China is, of course, part of the multilateral system, but within that system it does not occupy a position that is commensurate with its current strength; therefore, its participation in the international financial institutions is rather passive and its active expansion is likely to go through bilateral channels. For instance, China will complain about the role of the dollar and will promote the role of Special Drawing Rights (SDRs), but it is unlikely to allow the renminbi to become freely convertible because that would destroy the mechanism that has allowed the state to harvest the fruits of cheap Chinese labor through an undervalued currency. China will continue to maintain capital controls, but it will establish bilateral clearing accounts denominated in renminbi with countries like Brazil. This will diminish the status of the dollar as the international currency without replacing it.

To sum up: the world is facing a choice between two fundamentally different forms of economic organization, international capitalism and state capitalism. The former, represented by the United States, has broken down, and the latter, represented by China, is in the ascendant. The path of least resistance leads to the gradual disintegration of the international financial system as we know it. Yet a system of bilateral relations is liable to generate conflicts between states. A new multilateral system based on sounder principles needs to be invented. That would serve the best interests of both the United States and China, and, of course, the rest of the world.

While international cooperation is almost impossible to achieve on a piecemeal basis, it may be attainable in a grand bargain where the entire financial order. The emergence of the G20 as the primary forum of international cooperation and the peer review process adopted at the Pittsburgh meeting are steps in the right direction. But the G20 has to operate within the confines of the Articles of Association of the IMF because changing the Articles is a long, drawn-out process.

That is what a new Bretton Woods conference could accomplish in one fell swoop. It would reconstitute the IMF to better reflect the prevailing pecking order among states and revise its methods of operation. It would decide how to treat financial institutions that are too big to fail. And it would consider new rules to control capital movements. The total freedom of financial capital to move around internationally has proved to be a source of instability and needs to be curbed.

Above all, the international currency system needs to be reformed. The use of the dollar as the main international currency has produced dangerous imbalances. The dollar no longer enjoys the trust and confidence it once did, yet no other currency is in a position to take its place. There is a general flight from currencies into gold and other commodities and tangible assets. That is harmful because it keeps those assets out of productive use and stokes the fear of inflation.

The United States ought not to shy away from the wider use of SDRs. That should induce China to abandon pegging its currency to the dollar, and that would be the best way to reduce international imbalances. Since SDRs are denominated in several national currencies, no single currency would enjoy an unfair advantage.

The range of currencies included in SDRs would have to be widened, and some of the newly added currencies, which would include the renminbi, may not be fully convertible. Therefore the dollar could still reestablish itself as the preferred reserve currency, provided it is prudently managed.

One of the great advantages of SDRs is that they allow the international creation of credit. That would be particularly useful at times like the present. The credit could be directed to where it is most needed. That would be a great improvement over what is happening currently. A mechanism that allows rich countries that don't need additional reserves to transfer their allocations to those who need them is readily available and has already been used on a small scale.

The reorganization of the prevailing world order may have to extend beyond the financial system if we are to make progress in resolving issues such as global warming and nuclear proliferation.

It may have to involve the United Nations, especially regarding membership on the Security Council.

The process needs to be initiated by the United States, but China and other developing countries ought to participate in it as equals. They are reluctant members of the Bretton Woods institutions, which are dominated by countries that are no longer dominant. The rising powers need to be present at the creation of the new order to ensure that they will be active supporters of it.

Why should the United States initiate changes in a system of which it had has been the main beneficiary? Because the system cannot survive in its present form and the United States has more to lose if it is not in the forefront of reforming it. America lost a lot of power and influence during the Bush presidency. Without far-sighted leadership, the relative position of the United States is likely to continue eroding. The United States is still in a position to lead the world. It can no longer impose its will on others, as the Bush administration sought to do, but it could lead a cooperative effort that would involve not only the developed but also the developing world. This would reestablish American leadership in an acceptable form.

Why should China submit to a new multilateral system in view of the fact that it is set to emerge as the winner from the current turmoil? The answer is equally simple: in order to continue rising, it must make itself acceptable to the rest of the world. That means that it must move toward a more open society, combining an increased measure of individual freedom with the rule of law. Given the current military power relations, China can continue rising only in a peaceful environment in which the rest of the world willingly accepts the rise of China.

For the sake of a peaceful world, it is even more important that the United States finds its proper place in a new world order. A declining superpower losing both political and economic dominance while preserving military supremacy is a dangerous mix.

And, as I have tried to show, democracy is in deep trouble in America. The financial crisis has inflicted hardship on a population that does not like to face harsh reality. President Obama has deployed the confidence multiplier and claims to have contained the recession. If there is a double dip, the population will become susceptible to all kinds of fear mongering and populist demagoguery. If President Obama fails, the next administration will be sorely tempted to create some diversion from troubles at home and that could be very dangerous to the world.

President Obama has the right vision, but he needs to be more far-sighted. He believes in international cooperation rather than the Bush-Cheney idea that might is right. But he is preoccupied with many pressing problems. Reinventing the international financial system is not high on his agenda. Some of his economic advisers still seem to believe that the efficient market hypothesis is valid, except once in a hundred years. The financial institutions that have survived are in a stronger competitive position than ever before, and they will resist a systematic overhaul that would curb their powers. What is lacking is a general recognition that the system is broken and needs to be reinvented. That is why it would be so important that the theory of financial markets I have outlined in these lectures should gain wider acceptance.

The Chinese leadership would need to be even more farsighted than President Obama. They are in the driver's seat, and if they moved toward a more open society they would have to give up some of their privileges. Right now, the Chinese public is willing to subordinate individual freedom to political stability and economic advancement, but that may not continue indefinitely. Corruption is a big problem, and China needs the rule of law so that citizens can criticize the government and prevent it from abusing its powers.

Also, China needs to become a more open society in order to be acceptable to the rest of the world, which will never subordinate the freedom of the individual to the prosperity of the Chinese state. As China is becoming a world leader, it must learn to pay more attention to the opinion of the rest of the world. But all this may be happening too fast for the Chinese leadership to adjust to it. China is too accustomed to thinking of itself as the victim of imperialism to realize that it is beginning to occupy an imperialistic position. That is why it has such difficulties in dealing with Africa and its own ethnic minorities. I hope that the Chinese leadership will rise to the occasion. It is no exaggeration to say that the future of the world depends on it.

Thank you.

INDEX

George Soros is chairman of Soros Fund Management and is the founder of a global network of foundations dedicated to supporting open societies. He is the author of many best-selling books, most recently *The New Paradigm for Financial Markets*. He was born in Budapest and lives in New York City.

PUBLICAFFAIRS is a publishing house founded in 1997. It is a tribute to the standards, values, and flair of three persons who have served as mentors to countless reporters, writers, editors, and book people of all kinds, including me.

I. F. STONE, proprietor of *I. F. Stone's Weekly,* combined a commitment to the First Amendment with entrepreneurial zeal and reporting skill and became one of the great independent journalists in American history. At the age of eighty, Izzy published *The Trial of Socrates,* which was a national bestseller. He wrote the book after he taught himself ancient Greek.

BENJAMIN C. BRADLEE was for nearly thirty years the charismatic editorial leader of *The Washington Post*. It was Ben who gave the *Post* the range and courage to pursue such historic issues as Watergate. He supported his reporters with a tenacity that made them fearless, and it is no accident that so many became authors of influential, best-selling books.

ROBERT L. BERNSTEIN, the chief executive of Random House for more than a quarter century, guided one of the nation's premier publishing houses. Bob was personally responsible for many books of political dissent and argument that challenged tyranny around the globe. He is also the founder and was the longtime chair of Human Rights Watch, one of the most respected human rights organizations in the world.

. . .

For fifty years, the banner of Public Affairs Press was carried by its owner Morris B. Schnapper, who published Gandhi, Nasser, Toynbee, Truman, and about 1,500 other authors. In 1983 Schnapper was described by *The Washington Post* as "a redoubtable gadfly." His legacy will endure in the books to come.

Peter Osnos, *Founder and Editor-at-Large*